design your **self**

This book is dedicated to all humanity. We are all one family.
Let's love and respect each other and let's design and shape
a better, more enlightened world.

design your self

rethinking the way you live, love, work, and play

karim rashid

ReganBooks
An Imprint of HarperCollins*Publishers*

Love

Play

The new

YOU

The future is here and it is

beau

Not that many years ago, calculators were the size of a thick paperback book. Now we carry endless gigabytes of information on a computer half that size. More to the point, most of the technological breakthroughs we enjoy today we could not have imagined a decade ago. The world is changing, and everything that surrounds us is steadily becoming more user friendly, more designed, and more contemporary.

Within my lifetime, I will wake up in the morning to soothing sounds. The smart polarizing glass will go from black to clear. I will make my way to the bathroom on a floor that's just the right temperature. The bathroom will be fully automated; it will take my vital signs as I go about my business.

When I walk into the kitchen, the best possible cup of coffee will be waiting for me in the most comfortable mug ever designed, and it will be precisely the way I like it. The refrigerator will tell me what's fresh, and if I reach for something, it will provide recipes based on what's available.

The computer wallpaper tells me the time and what my day looks like. It tells me who I'm meeting and when, what the meeting is about, and who will be in attendance.

If I ask for music, I get music; news, I get news.

The lights will follow me back to the bedroom. The closet will open as I get ready to dress, and it will make suggestions about what I might wear. It will even remember who I'm meeting with and what I was wearing the last time I met with those people, and what I might consider today—according to the weather, of course.

As I make my way back into the living room; I notice that the vase has changed colors. That lets me know the water needs changing.

Before I leave, I put on a pair of high-performance shoes I ordered online.

When I leave, closing the door behind me, the house gets to work, cleaning itself.

I get into a car, and the electric seat is customized to my anatomy. Even the steering wheel is completely ergonomic—from just the touch of my hand it knows it's me and the engine starts and we're ready to roll.

The car asks me where I'm going and what I'd like to listen to.

When I get to the office, the doors sense my approach and open to let me through. My office chair is a dream, anthropomorphically attuned to my entire body.

If it's cold, the microfibers in my clothes warm up slightly so that I'm at exactly the temperature I find most comfortable.

When I go to lunch, I need nothing but an appetite. I don't carry a wallet. I don't have anything in my pockets. No keys, no cell phone, nothing. There's a microchip in my index finger that contains my credit card information, one in my earlobe that is a phone and another in my iris for visual communication. When I want to dial, I simply ask the chip to dial and I'm connected. Internet access is built into my anatomy.

If I have to travel, I will be picked up by a small electric car that checks me in en route to the airport. All I travel with is a small computer and a single change of clothes. The computer has everything I need on it: movies, books, design plans, calendars, music, and so on.

I arrive in a new city, hang up my self-cleaning clothes, change into my fresh outfit, and go to work, dinner, or play.

When I return to the hotel, the windows turn opaque and become video screens. Sleep no longer exists, there is only dream time.

When I wake up in the morning, the world is there to serve me so that I can be the best version of me I can be.

My desire is to see people living in our time, participating in our contemporary world, and delivered from nostalgia and antiquated notions. My hope is that we become conscious and sensorially attuned with this world, in this moment. If it is human nature to live in the past, we have to change it. To look back is to impede our forward momentum. There is nothing to be afraid of; we should embrace technology, allow progress to run its course, and *believe* how much better our lives can be. That is what I have set out to do. I want to change the world.

DESIGN THEORY (Why me?)

In the last twenty years, I have designed everything from snow shovels to teacups, watches to couches, mailboxes to martini glasses. When I first started designing, I had the idea that I wanted a product in every shop. I'm still working on that one, but I am proud to say I have designs not only at Bloomingdale's and museum shops but also at Costco and Target, which means that they are touching the lives of the broadest possible spectrum of people. In my life, in my work, and in my travels, I like to cross boundaries. I try to see the world from the inside out. I watch people use and live with products, with each other, and the space that surrounds them. I am fascinated with the interaction of people and things and the idea that I could make that interface more efficient, pleasurable, and seamless.

Design has a way of shaping people's lives, their behavior, sensibility, and psyche. As a designer, I have a special vantage point. I not only think about every aspect of our daily lives but I see several different ways we could do any one thing. I observe and analyze behavior, design, and the interface of the two. I am a shaper of everyday

I want to

change

the
world.

commodities and, as such, I hope to impart some of my findings and lead you to rethink where and how you live, even what and whom you live with. Sometimes it amounts to a good dose of common sense and, often, it is merely a question of changing your perspective. Always, it has to do with dedication. Perhaps because I have a multicultural background and grew up traveling, I never feel quite comfortable. This is simultaneously what stimulates me—gives me the impetus to design and change things—and what keeps me from conforming to any place, culture, or medium. I like feeling alien—like someone from another planet just observing and engaging in the human condition.

OBJECTIVITY

Designers have to be completely open minded, unbiased by race, aesthetics, religion, or any other kind of perspective. They must accept all they see and derive forms from abstraction. The reason artists are good at commenting on society is that they see the world as others don't. It is said that artists see the present while everyone else sees the past. Designers are able to see things that don't (yet) exist. That is my gift and one I don't take for granted. Very often a client will tell me that they are having trouble "seeing" a project that hasn't been built, that they need something to compare to. In order to create something new,

thinking outside

I have to make every effort to detach myself from references. This is something we should all work on. We need to try to be objective, to see everything as it is now, and to really live in a contemporary world.

As humans, we try to find keyholes for any incoming information. In order to understand, we make comparisons to what we already know, and this is an effective formula at some level. It is not, however, what we refer to as "thinking outside the box," which is what interests us as designers. What I design are things we already need (not things I predict needing in the future), and therein lies the challenge. If all my life I've been sitting down at a table with four legs and a chair with four legs with a plate surrounded by a fork on the left and a knife on the right, I will have a hard time inventing a new utensil. If I stick to what I know, I won't get past changing the number of prongs on a fork or making the edge of the knife more or less serrated. But if I step outside of history, habit, tradition, and what I already know, I might come up with an innovative solution.

Industrial design is somewhat limited in that we have to work within certain mandates—until couches can hover over the floor, we need to create something that can stand and balance. Until then, we are challenged to make it work. The same will be true of designing your self—you can't exactly start from scratch, and you will have some obstacles to work around, but the key is to find the fearlessness to push those boundaries. By changing a shape radically or using an unexpected color, we might find we live a happier,

the box

I believe that humans are on earth to **create.**

freer life. This goes from how we dress in the morning to the colors we surround ourselves with and the comfort of the car we get into every day. Many people admire the variety of colors in a field of flowers or the plumage of an exotic bird but would never dare to bring those colors into their home or wardrobe. Why?

If we didn't have fear, we would be a different society, certainly a different-looking one. My concern is that such fears are so prevalent that we don't even know we have them. Ask yourself why you have to have the couch where it is, the carpet arranged just so, with the coffee table in front of it, and a vase on the mantelpiece? Maybe it's a successful arrangement, tried and true for generations, but it's still worth considering. What if you moved the table to the side and left a flowing empty space in the center of the room?

What if you replaced the hard-edged rectangular table with an oval one that you wouldn't need to worry about kids running into? What if the color of your refrigerator door actually made you happy?

CREATIVITY

I believe that humans are on earth to create. I have recently been fascinated with the idea that we are all creative as children—all of our parents had our drawings prominently displayed around the house and we were encouraged to take colored markers, pencils, paints, and crayons to endless reams of white paper with wild abandon. Today, I notice that we continue to be fascinated with the way children see things, the associations that they make; even their "mistakes" are intriguing because they come from a very pure place, and yet, at a certain age, the promotion of the creative impulse stops. Once a child begins going to school, societal pressures start to take hold; acting a little "different" becomes a problem and children are pressured to conform. When I was six years old, I was hit on the left hand with a ruler for trying to write with it. Now, though it happens in more subtle ways, society still thwarts children's impulses to think, act, write, draw, sing, or behave in ways that stray from the norm. Hyperactivity is punished or, worse yet, medicated; it is no surprise that we grow up afraid to differ, afraid to express our true selves.

Ours is a man-made world—from computer technology to cooking—all these are creations, and we all have the potential to be creative if encouraged and free to be so. If our instincts to express ourselves were not suppressed, we would design our lives very differently, in more personal, individual, and expressive ways. What I'm here to tell you is that we have that freedom—in the United States and Canada, perhaps more than anywhere else in the world. This is where the

paper cup was invented. By simply rolling a piece of paper in a cone shape and sticking a base and a top on it, we invented takeout, and with that came the idea that you could eat anything, anywhere, anytime. The concept spread swiftly around the world, and now we take for granted that we can eat Indian, Mexican, or Japanese food on any given night of the week, anywhere we want to take it, without even seeing the restaurant. It doesn't seem like a revolutionary idea now, but it's just one of the many innovations that's taken hold around the world and contributed to our progressive casualization.

CASUALIZATION

Over the years—and particularly in my travels—I have witnessed the world changing exponentially. Youth culture is informed by technology and, in turn, young people are interested in participating globally. Their cross-cultural positioning and views extend to an open-mindedness to change that is extremely encouraging. Our ultimate goal should be to become unbiased and completely free to express ourselves.

The paper cup I mentioned, designed in the 1930s, shows how design changes our lives. It was seminal to the fast-food industry, but it also paved the way for less obvious cultural shifts. In Japan it was considered unorthodox to eat or drink on the street in public, but over the last five years I have observed a significant change. Starbucks opened in Shibuya (the Times Square of Tokyo), and now I see young people taking out their coffees and drinking them on the street for the first time in Japanese history. Casualization is a metaphor for freedom of thinking, likes and dislikes—for not being programmed to think a certain way or have prefabricated tastes.

EFFICIENCY/STREAMLINING/FLUIDITY

Whatever people say about this trend, the direction we're taking, it is the route of efficiency. Eliminating formalities saves time and allows for greater mobility. Technology is at the forefront of this shift. Think about the way we work. More and more people work from home (or elsewhere). We may be tied to our computers but we are not necessarily stuck in an office or chained to a desk. Laptops allow us to work anywhere and anytime we want, which means we are also designing our own time. Many of us are already working on a global clock, in "Internet time," which is the most fluid of all.

CONFIDENCE/FREEDOM/ENTREPRENEURSHIP

The United States has pioneered this liberating tendency. Every day we come closer to living exactly the life we want. If we are empowered by self-confidence, there is really no limit to what we can do. Entrepreneurship is an American invention; nowhere in the world are individuals so encouraged to pursue their dreams. In Japan, for instance, until recently there were no independent designers. Students had to be discouraged from working for large corporations, and slowly there began to be some small start-ups. In the United States the ratio of small to large business is fifty-fifty. And this individual freedom not only applies to your work, but the spirit of entrepreneurship permeates

It takes a sense of freedom to realize your dreams.

Ask Yourself:

What are my strengths?
What can I contribute?
What do I enjoy?

everything—from what you study to what you eat to how you dress, speak, or decorate your home.

Get to the bottom of that in your work, your relationships, and every other aspect of your life. Think of it as a trajectory and map it out.

DESIGN vs. CRAFT

The difference between "design" and "craft" lies in the intention. To design is to plan, to develop a set of criteria, and to map something out. A craftsman starts with the material, a piece of wood, for example, and works around its knots to fashion a shape. A designer, on the other hand, has to devise a complete plan. Prior to execution there are numerous stages: from sketches to drawings, computer renderings to full-scale models. Revisions are made throughout, and nothing is left to chance.

When I first meet with a client, I have many ideas because at that moment I am most excited and inspired by the new subject. I then go to my office and sketch ideas for the project immediately for an hour before I forget them.

Craft is incidental. Design generally is not. If there is an accidental outcome, it is because it springs from the subconscious. In designing something you exercise control over it. When I say you can design your self, I mean it. You have full control. There is no need to float when you can steer your way. The principles of design are there to guide you, and, as you will see, they can be applied to all aspects of your life.

Design is for
EVERYONE!

DESIGNOCRACY

From forty-dollar stackable chairs to luxury hotels, there is very little I haven't designed (yet). I create with people in mind and am constantly trying to make the world better, simpler, more organized, contemporary, streamlined, and pleasant. I care not only about the way things work but also how they look, smell, and feel.

Although I enjoy designing everything, I am particularly interested in FMCGs (fast-moving consumer goods). I try to design objects that are both useful and affordable. I firmly believe that design is for everyone and I have made Designocracy my mission in life. I am less concerned about keeping design in museums than I am in seeing it proliferated. Design may be about turning toasters and vacuum cleaners into objects of consumer desire, but the primary purpose of design is to impact the way we live. In order to do that, it must be accessible. I have seen people literally transformed by their environment; I have witnessed order come from chaos.

We each define and design our own lives. We design the way we get out of bed in the morning. We design our wardrobes, the food we eat, the work we do, and the way we relate to others. Now imagine taking every aspect of your life and looking at it the way I approach a new project.

Ask yourself:

How can we make this work?   More pleasurable?

More responsive to our needs?   More fun?

More efficient?   More fulfilling?

More beautiful?   More meaningful?

That is what this book is about. It is designed to help you rethink the way you live, love, work, play, eat, sleep, etc. I've put it together over a lifetime and it belongs to everyone I have ever met: the people who loved me, those who insulted me, and those who praised me. The ones who gave me a chance to prove myself and those who didn't. The ones who treated me harshly and those who were kind. We are all shaped and altered by every experience. I hope this book proves to be such an experience for you and that it inspires you to become your own best design.

WHO IS KARIM

Before I go on to suggest how to redesign your life, I should probably tell you a little about myself—so you know where I'm coming from...

I was born in Cairo in 1960, to an Egyptian father and an English mother. He was a painter and a set designer working on his master's degree in Paris. She was a tourist, visiting from London. They met in the subway, fell in love, and were soon married. They lived in Rome, London, back in Paris, and then settled in my father's native Cairo, where they had two children: my older brother and me. My sister was born in Canada eight years later.

To say we settled is a bit of an overstatement. As a painter, my father was invited to exhibit his work in cities all over the world and it seemed as if we were always in motion. As a family, we went to Alexandria, Rome, Paris, and London. "There is nothing that expands the mind like traveling," my father used to say. This explained why he insisted on bringing us along even if it meant missing a week or two of school. "Keep your eyes and ears open and you'll learn far more than you will in class." He would take me out into foreign streets, carrying sketchpads and pencils. "Draw what you see," he would repeat tirelessly, "not what you think you see." His advice taught me to really look at things.

That was my early childhood—different places, different cultures, and different languages. We went from city to city, visiting museums, wandering the streets, admiring the architecture. As a result, I developed an almost exclusively urban sensibility. I loved cities. I loved buildings. I loved design. Nature, on the other hand, didn't interest me in the least. Houses, buildings, and bridges were things that had been willed to life.

I began to draw obsessively. I sketched churches, monuments, and other objects. I sketched them as they were but also as I would have liked them to be. Sometimes I made the windows a little larger, or added skylights, to bring the sun indoors. Sometimes I'd smooth out all the hard edges, creating a gentler and more inviting environment.

My parents were delighted with my entrancement, at least initially, but before long they began to worry. I would sketch for hours at a time, and I was so intensely focused that the world around me disappeared. When I was five our family went to Canada aboard the *Queen Elizabeth II*. On the way over, the ship's staff organized an art contest for the 300 children on board. Most of the kids turned to nature for inspiration—dolphins, sunsets, islands—but my subject was

Everything in my drawings was better than it was

luggage: big, rectangular suitcases, piled on top of each other, like leather building blocks. I took first prize for my efforts and was deeply affected, not so much because I had won but because my work had been validated by strangers for the first time.

I began to take sketching more seriously, and I think that in some ways that shipboard experience helped determine the course of my life. I was lucky. I had found something I loved at a very young age and I kept at it. I lost myself in this wonderful, limitless world. I began to draw almost exclusively from my imagination. There was a period when all I drew were houses. I would draw the exterior, the interior, the family inside it, each of the rooms, and every detail in each room,

down to the flatware on the dining room table. Everything in my
drawings was better than it was in real life. I was fixated on
improving things.

In 1967, shortly before my seventh birthday, my family moved to
Canada. My father had a few weeks before he had to report to his
new job at the Canadian Broadcasting Corporation, so he took us to
see Expo 67, which had opened in Montreal only a few months earlier.
The theme of the fair was "Man and His World," a futuristic wonderland.
There was Habitat, the most exhilarating housing development the
world had ever seen. Designed by Canadian architect Moshe Sadie,
it consisted of 158 prefabricated rectangular houses stacked on top of
each other to form an ersatz pyramid. The Dutch had designed a

in real life. I was fixated on improving things.

"space-frame" building made out of 57,000 pieces of aluminum
tubing, and the Germans created a massive tent made of steel mesh
and steel girders that covered the equivalent of an entire city block.
The United States was represented by Buckminster Fuller and one of
his famous geodesic domes. The structure was twenty stories high
and consisted entirely of triangles and hexagons, curved to form
perfect arcs. There were plenty of other eye-catching designs—
structures made entirely of wooden crossbeams, interconnecting
cubes, polygons, sheets of glass and aluminum, and cardboard that
looked like stone. They left an indelible impression—this was what I
was going to do with my life.

In 1971, when I was eleven, my father took the family to New York to see a design show at the Museum of Modern Art. It was called the New Domestic Landscape, and it featured the work of some of Italy's most forward-thinking architects and designers. It was astonishing. They were using polyurethane and pressed rubber and foam to create furniture that resembled pop art. I saw a couch that looked like a set of giant red lips; a cactus-shaped clothes stand; chairs designed to resemble giant boulders; a rug that passed for a lawn. I wasn't sure I liked everything I saw, but I was inspired. I realized that anything I could imagine, I could create.

In high school I found most of my classes boring, so I turned to other interests. I started a newspaper, became the school's self-appointed music impresario, launched a radio station, and started an art club. When I graduated, a year early, I went to study industrial design at Carleton University in Ottawa. Four years later, I flew to Naples to do graduate studies and ended up spending the entire year working at the Rodolfo Bonetto Studio in Milan. I helped design a stereo television, worked on an industrial espresso machine for La Cimbali (that still exists in restaurants and cafes worldwide), and designed a few lamps that looked only vaguely like lighting. I designed furniture and dashboards for Fiat.

The following summer I returned to Canada and went to work for KAN Industrial Designers, where I spent the next seven years of my life. I designed mailboxes for Canada Post, a laptop for Toshiba, an electric drill and various electric kettles for Black & Decker, train seats, and an information kiosk for Union Station in Toronto.

During my time at KAN I started a fashion company with two

I felt that **DESIGN SHOULD ASPIRE** to the realm of great art.

architect friends. Clothing design allowed for greater creative freedom than industrial design, and the clothes we made won numerous awards and sold in stores from Toronto to New York, Los Angeles, Miami, and Chicago.

For Black & Decker, I also designed the True Temper snow shovel. It was one of the first plastic snow shovels ever made: Until then, they were constructed almost exclusively of sheet metal and wood. It went on to become a huge success, selling millions of units. I remember walking home during an early winter snowfall and seeing people clearing their driveways with my shovel. It was an exhilarating experience. The shovel worked. It was light, colorful, and less noisy than metal shovels—and it was cheap. It was a very democratic product, accessible to all, and it was everywhere I looked.

In 1990, I left KAN for a teaching job at the Ontario College of Art in Toronto. I had worked on dozens of projects, and I had enjoyed the experience, but it had left me feeling like an engineer rather than a designer. I felt that design should aspire to the realm of great art, and

Do what you **believe**

this is what I tried to impress upon my students. I wanted them to reach, even overreach!

The following year I heard that the Rhode Island School of Design, one of the most reputable design schools in America, had a full-time opening for an assistant professor. I didn't even know where Rhode Island was, but I eventually located the school and made my way across the border with my portfolio under my arm.

I got the job, and the school helped me secure a visa. Before I knew it, I had packed up my life and found myself living in the United States. I didn't know a soul in Providence, and on my very first day I went out and found a spacious loft in the heart of downtown. I thought I'd been very lucky until I realized that, in those days, downtown Providence was a ghost town. At nightfall, people went home and I felt like the last man on earth. My apartment was broken into twice and I was held up at gunpoint. I began to wonder whether I had made a big mistake.

I loved teaching and have a great passion for nurturing and educating students, but at the end of the year I decided to take a chance on New York City. I applied for a teaching job at Parsons, was hired, and lost the job after a scant three days. Apparently, when they got around to talking to the faculty at Rhode Island, they were told that I had been teaching theory and philosophy, not design, as I'd been hired to do, and that that my conceptual methods didn't fit in with the school's more traditional approach to the craft of design. I then applied to the Pratt Institute, also in Manhattan, and thanks largely to Peter Barna, the school's chair at the time, they hired me on the spot. "I heard you were a troublemaker," he told me. "Well, that's exactly what we're looking for." There was a lesson in this: Do what you believe and you will end up where you belong.

I found a small loft without a kitchen or bathroom and settled in to teach two days a week. The rest of the time I tried to sell myself as a designer. I spent a lot of time on Amtrak visiting literally hundreds of companies: from La-Z-Boy to Ethan Allen to Gillette. I was full of ideas, but no one was interested. The small companies found my ideas too radical, and the larger companies didn't even entertain them: They already had plenty of designers on the payroll, and my credentials— a professor with a few designs to his credit—didn't impress them. From time to time, however, someone would express a modicum of interest in one of my ideas, and they'd ask me to sketch a little

and you will end up
where you belong.

something for them, so they could get a better handle on what I was talking about. I would send them thirty sketches, without remuneration, and if I didn't hear back I'd send them thirty more.

Finally, a small company in Santa Fe took a chance on me. The company was Nambe, and they were known primarily for their tabletop accessories. This time I decided to overprepare, and several students helped me put together a portfolio of computer renderings. We created an infinite variety of candlesticks, vases, bowls, and dishes, and the representatives were sufficiently impressed to want to take a look at the actual products. Unfortunately, I was forced to explain that the products didn't exist. Back in those days, just twelve years ago, design software was still in its infancy, and I'd been forced to create the products on a computer screen and photograph the actual screen. The products only looked real, but I knew I could make them come to life and I assured the people at Nambe that I would deliver on my promise.

I went home from Santa Fe with a check in my hand. A year later I walked into Bloomingdale's, and there they were, for sale: my Ellipses vases, my Nova candlesticks, my "kissing" salt and pepper shakers. I was ecstatic. The collection started selling about five million dollars worth of units a year, and I've designed more than 300 products for Nambe since, six of which are in museum collections today.

Leave no stone
unturned.

My next job was for Umbra, a company with offices in Toronto. I had contacted them while I was in Rhode Island and had sent them so many sketches and proposals that they began to reject them without so much as the courtesy of a cover letter. In 1995 I went to see them in person. They asked me to design a simple wastebasket, but they had some caveats: It had to be relatively low to the ground, and it had to be inexpensive. I wasn't crazy about the height limitations but I realized I could make the basket look higher if I added handles, giving it a nicely rounded, swooping shape. The raised sides also made the wastebasket a tempting target: I imagined people "dunking" their trash from across the room.

The finished product was made of high-impact virgin polypropylene, and it looked kind of sexy. It was also inexpensive. The Garbo (a play on Greta Garbo and garbage) sold for around eight dollars, and at that affordable price the company moved more than four million units. It was good for them and good for me. It looked as if I might have a career after all. As one critic put it, "Karim built a better trash can and the world beat a path to his door."

An aside to note is that the name of that wastebasket turned out to be almost as important as the design itself: It made a garbage can sound attractive. And this is a very important lesson to consider as you go through the book. Think about every aspect of your life—your daily experiences as well as the more exceptional ones—pay attention, and leave no stone unturned. Sometimes it's a subtle change of perspective or the very detail you might have overlooked that makes all the difference.

Live

- Home
- Diet
- Dematerialization
- Fitness

The mantra of your domestic landscape should be:

Peace, Tranquility, Fluidity, and Inspiration.

The philosopher Martin Heidegger wrote a treatise called *Bauen Wohnen Denken* (Building Dwelling Thinking) where he explains that the core of the German word *bauen* (hence also the English word *build*) means "to dwell." To build is to dwell. Heidegger stipulated that what we build (how we dwell) is how we form a paradigm for our aesthetic views. That is, the way that we create our buildings, the way we think them beautiful, is the philosophy of beauty that permeates our lives.

The mantra of your domestic landscape should be: Peace, Tranquility, Fluidity, and Inspiration. Your domestic environment should be characterized by positive energy, heightened experiences, and contemporary design. It should be arranged to provide the highest level of comfort and spiritual well-being. It should be a place for new and contemporary experiences—to enjoy, relax, socialize, work, and engage in new and memorable experiences.

Ideally, every space that surrounds you should create a sensual envelopment. By this I mean that they should be soft, curved, and conceptual. They should engage technology, striking visuals, textures, and a multitude of colors while remaining simple, streamlined, and uncluttered.

Rounded edges and rooms that are soft in every possible way—from the lighting to sound, from tactile

IMAGINE

materials that give to the complete absence of sharp edges—provoke a more human-friendly living environment. Think of the adobe house. This is not such a radical idea; it's just that we've been locked into a Carthesian grid—the grid of modernism—for so long that we can't seem to escape it.

Whether it's a house or an apartment, we begin with a box and fit everything into it: a box within a box within a box. Think about how that extends to the outside too, the block you live on, the neighborhood, the demarcations of highways, train tracks, and so on. Think how liberating it would be to remove the hard edges and make everything more seamless. Next time you're on a plane, look down at that grid and think whether it is really the ideal way for us to live. Imagine every line a curve.

Why make a juncture when you can be seamless?

every line a curve.

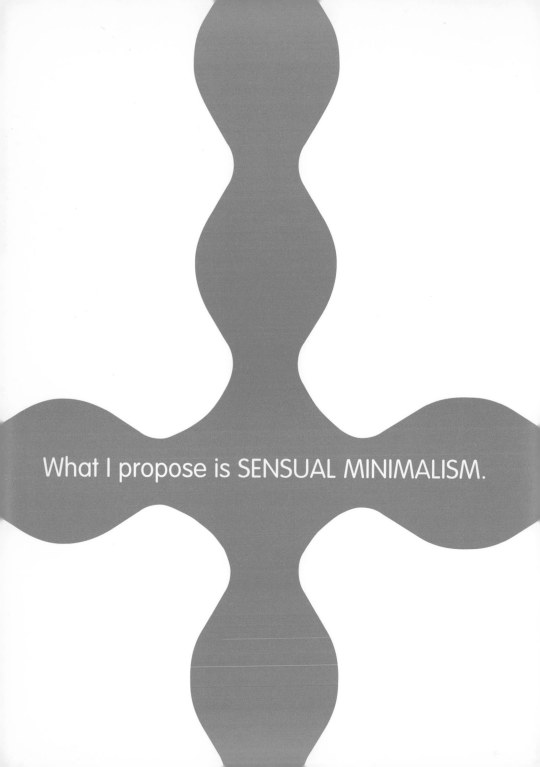

What I propose is SENSUAL MINIMALISM.

Corners are unnecessary. They are a point of friction, a place where dust collects. Think again of the plane, the inside of it this time, it's angleless interior. Think about the comforting cocoonlike feeling it evokes. The absence of corners and right angles makes for a more casual and amorphous space. There are no right angles in nature. We know we find comfort in bean bags and womblike spaces. Why fight it?

What I propose is sensual minimalism or sensualism. All objects have a semantic language—they speak to us. Forms, lines, colors, and textures communicate with our senses and form our daily experiences. I believe that it is important not to overembellish objects and to keep a certain truth to a product, but I also think that objects need to touch our sensual side, elevate our experiences, and be more human. Colors that are easy on the senses, materials that give, surfaces that are tactile, and shapes that are soft are what we should surround ourselves with.

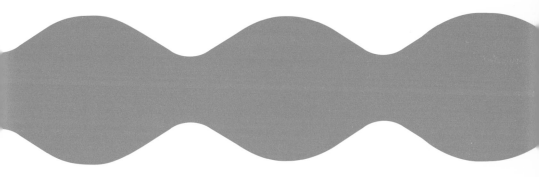

They enhance our experience of the material world and, together, make for a smoother, more seamless existence. My interest in sensualizing our physical material world is inherently linked with love and desire.

For all the reasons I have mentioned, children love my spaces. The absence of sharp angles and the cacophony of color make them more appealing. They have nothing to worry about there, no sharp edges, nothing too fragile. Everything is more tactile and more human. They can equally run and roll through the space. The space is open and unfettered by the past so children move with fluidity and without fear.

Children respond to platonic forms that are pure, not decorative extensions of history. There are no pre-associations in my spaces and this is very liberating for them and for us. **We shouldn't dwell in the past.** Instead, we should try to eliminate unnecessary historical references, rid our spaces of any superfluous objects, and use technology to make it as efficient as possible—while making every effort to maintain shapes and spaces that are soft, fluid, and seamless.

create open space
that is transformable and reconfigurable.

Ideally, our home should be one large open space that is transformable and reconfigurable, and allows objects and furniture to breathe and to shape the personality of the interior. Feng shui tells us to pay attention to the flow of energy within a space, and, in a sense, it's even simpler than that. We could make our own navigation of space so much easier if we eliminated unnecessary walls, doors, angles, and other obstacles. With the possible exception of bedrooms and bathrooms, all rooms can really be one.

Don't be afraid of color.

I have a loft and there you really flow thorough the space—there are no demarcation lines between kitchen, dining, living, loving, cooking, working, and playing "rooms." All these different areas share—and therefore maximize—air and light. They are perfectly seamless. I rearrange the furniture once a week so the place always looks fresh and new and try to add (or change) colors at every opportunity.

Our home (I live with my wife Megan, who is a painter) is like a large white canvas with accents of strong positive colors. We have white walls *and* white floors so verticals and horizontals blend into one fluid dimension. With less of an interruption between the floor and the ceiling, we feel less constrained. We have large windows so that the whole apartment basks in sunlight.

White evokes calm while accents of vibrant glowing colors awaken and elevate. **I love color and I'm not afraid of it.** I use it in an artistic

You have the power to

CHAN

way, to express myself. Color is a way of dealing with and touching our innermost emotions (and I will come back to this point). I love techno colors, colors that have the vibrancy and energy of our digital world. The colors I use imbue the space with a plethora of positive energy. My walls and floors are white so they reflect light and accentuate every color I add. I have a yellow mixing table; various types of seating in bright orange, hot pink, and lime green; multicolored digipop cabinets; and amoeba-shaped carpets in a veritable rainbow of varieties.

I have used wallpapers in several large-scale projects: the Semiramis Hotel in Athens, the Nooch restaurant in Singapore, the Future Design House in Cologne, and the Mind Body Seoul House in Korea. I am using my Digital Nature Collection designed for Wolf-Gordon for two hotels in England and a restaurant in Moscow. This gives the walls

Look around your space.

texture, shape, color, and newfound volume. It also makes them durable and easy to clean, which is perfect for commercial applications, as well as for the home.

In these interiors I used wallpaper to achieve another dimension but also ended up with a highly durable surface. Most wall coverings on the market keep repeating antiquated patterns that have no meaning in the modus of our time. Most wallpaper designs out there are very conservative, so I wanted to inject some new technographic ideas that are strong and speak about the age in which we live. Avoid dated wallpaper. If you're afraid you'll get bored with it, know that you can change it. It's not much more complicated than giving a room a fresh coat of paint.

As I will continue to repeat throughout the book, you have the power to *change*. Anything you want; for example, of all the pieces of furniture I've mentioned in my loft, absolutely nothing needs to stay where it is. The space is completely reconfigurable and totally dynamic. To achieve this it helps to have multiuse furniture. I have a semicircular couch that incorporates a coffee table or ottoman within its shape. It is equally usable as a deep couch or a narrower one with a removable part to put, your feet, a tray, or books on. Alternately, another person can sit on it facing the others. I have shelves that can stack in different shapes and heights to accommodate different spaces and functions. I designed a child's seat that doubles as a storage container for children's toys. I've made dinnerware in which all the parts of a setting slot perfectly into one another and another where containers join to form an entire landscape. I even have shoes with removable parts.

Another advantage of multiuse furnishings is that they mean you can live with less. If your dining table can double as a desk, you've saved yourself a lot of space. Throughout the book we will revisit the notion of **ADDITION BY SUBTRACTION** whereby you can have more with less. There are several measures you can take to pare down that will immediately give you more—whether it's space, time, or energy. To begin with, it is imperative that you remove all the possible clutter in your home (we'll get to the clutter in your mind later). Getting rid of excess clothing, objects, souvenirs, old newspapers, radios that don't work, shoes you don't wear, or misguided presents people have given you will prove extremely liberating. For this reason, I have dedicated the next chapter to this very process—dematerialization. In the meantime, while you consider your domestic environment, start thinking about what you might be able to live without. As of today, bring nothing in unless you're prepared to part with something else.

In addition to being hyperpractical and

efficient, all areas of the house should...

Look around your space. What do your surfaces look like? Are shelves overflowing with books? Do you have a hard time closing your closet door? Are your kitchen drawers brimming with things you had nowhere else to put? Are you hoarding mountains of half-read newspapers and magazines? One at a time, look at all the spaces that are collecting junk, mail or otherwise. Of course, you won't be able to get rid of everything right now, but you can start by considering these three essential measures:

1. **Set up systems to address the clutter as it makes its way into your space** (have dedicated places for incoming mail, a stack for new magazines, well-organized files for your paperwork, recycling containers, etc.).

2. **Devise some preventive measures** (read online, cancel any unnecessary subscriptions, ask to be taken off catalog mailing lists, and save some trees)!

3. **And, yes, throw some of that stuff away.**

For example, one problem most of us share is that we all get way too much mail. Finding a place for it is key. First, establish a convenient place to sort it. Throw away as much as possible in the first round and have a recycling container waiting nearby. Don't open bills until you're ready to pay them and file away what statements you can. Instead of letting mail accumulate, get in your way, and subtly wear you down, set it aside. Create a place and time for it, make yourself a cup of tea, put on some music, and focus on it all at once. Make different piles for what

Seamless space.

you need to simply file (statements, etc.), what you need to address, and what you need to pay. Once you have places set up for these three things, the mail won't get out of hand and the prospect of sorting it and paying bills will seem much less daunting next time around.

Remember that it is not just the mess of excess itself, it's the effect that it has on your psyche. This is why it's important to address it *now*. What you want to achieve in your space is peace and tranquility and, even if you can't tear down walls and round all your edges, this is something anyone can—and everyone should—do.

In addition to being hyperpractical and efficient, all areas of the house should *inspire*. The kitchen should make you want to cook, entertain, and experiment. A desk should promote focus, attention, and enjoyment of the task at hand. Your couch should literally invite you to dive in. Light should resemble daylight. Colors should wake you up in the morning and follow you throughout the day. Music should surround you, and all telephone ringers and alarm clocks should be sounds you want to hear. Scents are powerful tools, too. How many times have you noticed a wonderful smell in a shop, a garden, or someone's home and thought how nice it would be to live with it? Like music, you should have different scents for different occasions, moods, and times of day.

By the same token, the two rooms with particular functions should be perfectly geared to them. The bedroom should be just what it sounds like: a room with a bed in it, that's it. The primary function of this room is sleeping (and dreaming) so keep it *simple*. Go there now, and look around. Is there anything you could move elsewhere that would make it a more peaceful place? Anything there that you might find stressful? Have you made the bed? Before you go to sleep tonight, try to do at least one thing that might improve the quality of your dreams (we will come back to this later in the book).

The bathroom has more complex functions and is the most obvious place where new technologies should be applied. I love the bathroom and I can't help thinking how much more it could be. At the very least, what we need are rubber baths, watertight rubber floors. We should also have highly adaptable lighting that can imitate daylight, halogen, fluorescent, disco, or moonlight at the flick of a switch. Ideally, we would have "smart" bathrooms that diagnose our health through our waste; floors that tell us our weight, heartbeat, and blood pressure; a mirror that tracks our vital signs and gives us digital feedback on our health and appearance. Sinks, toilets, lights—everything should be automatic (like the bathroom in my house) and require no hand contact whatsoever. The more we make our spaces efficient and seamless, the more room we will have to think and do what we really want.

Try this now.
Become hypersensitive to this particular moment, the **smell**, the **touch**, the **feeling**, the **sight**, the **sound**, the **taste**.

Focus on this moment and realize that everything in front of you is part of rising above thoughts—the ones that take you somewhere else, into the past. When we start thinking of issues or conditions that have to do with another place, they are generally concerned with our history or a place that is not part of the moment. The moment is here and it is now, and that is true liberation and true freedom. Be aware of when you are thinking about the past, be very conscious when you are thinking about the future, then stop that thought and think about *now*, this moment, reading these words. Think about the chair you are sitting in; the space around you; the humidity; the temperature; the taste on your lips; the view; the feeling of the book in your hands; the feeling of the clothes against your skin; your feet, and the ground they are touching, how they feel in your shoes or socks; the light. Is it in your eyes? Is it bright or dark? Fluorescent or incandescent?

When you consider all this you have more energy, you realize that you are alive, that you are present, that you exist, that you are part of the world around you, and that you are touching and being in that context, that room, the physical materials surrounding you. Try to realize your consciousness, realize that you are alive, breathing, and participating in this beautiful physical world that we have created. That you are part of everyone else, an extension of that space, and that space is in turn an extension of another space: your chair touches the floor that touches the building that touches the ground that touches the roads, the trees, other cities, the ocean, the atmosphere, the universe, and the cosmos. You are an intrinsic part of this.

Here are my thirty most important recommendations for the home:

1. Create large white spaces with accents of strong positive colors.

2. Knock down walls that are not structural and open up spaces as much as possible.

3. No visible books, magazines, CDs, or clutter. No bookshelves.

4. Have less but better furniture. Try to substitute two or three pieces with one.

5. Flat surfaces accumulate things, so have a small side table near the entrance for keys, mp3 players, mobile phones, etc.

6. Put all your chargers in one place—with one surge protector—and always make sure everything is fully charged.

7. Try to consolidate all your technology so that your computer, TV, and stereo are all of a piece.

8. Have a plasma screen or watch a projection TV.

9. Use warm, soft, but high-performance materials.

10. Embrace (don't fear) technology.

11. All kitchen products should be hidden. The kitchen should be bare and beautiful. Only the most sensual and artistic designs should be on display. All other gadgets need to be hidden.

12. Impose order.
Line everything up perfectly: vases, objects, books, stereo equipment. Order inspires. Order is Zen. Order is relaxing.

13. Don't be a pack rat: recycle newspapers and magzines as soon as you're done reading them. Better yet, read them online.

14. Avoid curtains. They are dirt and dust collectors and make spaces look smaller with added bulk and weight. Use seamless mesh blinds instead.

15. Use materials that are easy to clean and that age well. Plastic floors (laminates, vinyl sheeting, or artificial rubber) are lightweight and inexpensive materials that wear well and are more resistant to scratches and staining.

16. Colored glass looks great in bathrooms; it plays with the changing light.

17. **Use dimmer switches** throughout the house and incandescent light over fluorescent. Halogen bulbs are also nice. Put everything on timers and sensors.

18. **Use color to express yourself.** Don't be afraid of that bright orange chair. Paint your wall lime green. Be brave when it comes to carpets, countertops, and tables. Color is beautiful, and it's all about self-expression. Be yourself.

19. Do not buy useless, kitschy souvenirs.

Do you really need a sombrero from Puerto Vallarta? If you bring something into your home, make sure it has meaning.

20. **Wallpaper is wonderful.** It lasts longer than paint and is easy to clean and replace.

21. **Wall-to-wall carpeting is warm**, easy to maintain, pleasurable, soft, and friendly.

22. Use biodegradable and natural cleaning products.

23. **Anytime you buy something for your home, get rid of something else.** Seek *balance*. People tend to accumulate far more than they need. Buy a vase; get rid of a vase.

24. **If you're moving to a new place, look for lots of light.** Daylight is essential to positive thinking and your well-being. If you're not moving, look for ways to maximize the light you have: skylights, enlarged windows, and so on.

25. **Make do with less.** And make sure you really want what you're buying. I'm not anti-consumption per se, but I think it's essential to consume with awareness. Buy only what you need.

26. **Avoid sharp edges.** Let your space flow.

27. **Addition by subtraction.** This is one of my pet theories, and it's really very simple. You get rid of things you don't want and your life becomes fuller. Less becomes more; the things you do keep become more valuable.

28. Make your space reconfigurable.

29. **You don't need storage space.** If something is stashed away, you're not using it. Get rid of it.

30. Be sure the next thing you buy has more than one use.

DEMATERI

ALIZATION

Dematerialization—whether getting rid of superfluous objects, stresses, excess weight, or baggage—is one of the most immediate ways you can impact your daily life. Generally speaking, downsizing refers to eliminating anything in your life that is stressful, unnecessarily time consuming, or detrimental. This can be interpreted in various ways, whether it is the relatively simple elimination of material things or the more difficult issue of changing our habits to improve our health and fitness. Just as too many objects cluttering our space can literally get in our way, so can hoarding, overeating, and other compulsive behavior impede our progress and interfere with our quality of life.

Though it may seem like a paradox, I believe we can add to our lives by subtracting, especially by reducing our consumption. In my theory of addition by subtraction, less can ultimately be more. And I am not suggesting a minimalist or reductive approach but, instead, a way of enriching one's life and experiences through beautiful things, the things that we love. What I propose is that we learn to edit our choices and thereby create the most important luxury of the twenty-first century: *time*. If we can remove banalities, frustrations, and time-consuming scenarios, we can spend more time thinking, creating, loving, being, and fulfilling our dreams. As we achieve this, our time takes on a more constructive, more contributive, role. We will ultimately be happier because we will no longer be bombarded with pettiness, bogged down with mediocrity, or numbed by banal experiences. By subtracting we can grow.

By no means am I advocating that we should not be buying or having things. I firmly believe that we should be hyperconscious of the things we surround ourselves with—either love and enjoy them or do without them. Objects denote our time, place, and relationship with the outside world and others. They can have a phenomenal relationship with our daily lives and, at the same time, they can become perpetual obstacles, complicating our lives and creating stress. It is essential that we learn to identify what is most important and beneficial to us and differentiate it from what we can live without. This goes for all aspects of our lives, whether it's the clutter under our desks, a social calendar full of obligations, or the excess thoughts in our heads.

The present is all we have and the more we are surrounded by it, the more alive we are.

When I look around my personal environment, my house, my office, even my car, I ask myself whether everything there has a meaning. Is it relevant to my time? Do I have anything that really has no significance to me, such as gifts I was given, mistaken purchases, or things? Is there anything there that I have been keeping over time, sometimes to the point of not even seeing it anymore? I call these "accumulated meaningless commodities."

Do I need these things?

The answer is (probably) *no.*
Ask yourself three simple questions:

1. Do they provide an important or reliable function or performance in my home?

2. Do they have real meaning for me? Am I emotionally connected to them?

3. Do they add beauty to my life?

Of course, the first question is simple. If I have a stereo, does it play music? It may play music, but does it do its job really well? Do I love music? Do I enjoy listening to music? If I do, is that stereo giving me the quality of sound I should have, considering my passion for music? Does the stereo function well—is it easy to use? Is its performance, quality, and technology exceptional? Is it seamless, simple, and direct? The reason I ask these questions is that I am always amazed to find the amount of technology that people have in their homes that is completely outdated and has no real value.

"Why keep it?" is the bigger question. Technology has become so accessible and incredibly inexpensive, almost disposable. Today, high-tech products have an eleven-month shelf life, meaning they are dated and better technology usually supersedes them within that time frame. Yet some of us hang on to these products thinking they are valuable, because we have invested so much in them already.

Sometimes garbage is just garbage.

My mother, for example, holds on to a computer from 1989 because it is "a computer," which means to her that it must be valuable. It is not—it has no more value than an old suit she would donate to the nearest Salvation Army without hesitation. If she were really concerned about value, she should be thinking about it in terms of time as well as money.

The trouble she has turning it on, how often she has to call someone for help, or the fact that she can't get a printer that's compatible are all factors to be considered.

Do you have a computer that doesn't turn on, a toaster that won't pop, a car door that gets jammed one out of three times you close it? You have to begin thinking about these things in terms of what they take out of you and your precious time. Even if you spend five minutes a day plugging and unplugging, shaking or banging something until it works, remember this takes its toll on you and is cumulatively an enormous waste of time, not to mention an unnecessary source of stress. If nine times out of ten you receive a file that you have trouble opening and need it sent again or to convert it to your outdated system, it's probably time for an upgrade.

I notice this with cars as well. Everyone's car has its little quirks, often ones only their owner has learned to contend with, but there comes a time when they, too, start taking their toll—on your time, on your peace of mind, on your day. People who commute every day by car should put as much of their disposable income into their car as possible. If you spend two to four hours a day, your car should be like your living room. In other words, if you are going to spend so much time with something (remember, life is short), it should be the best experience possible—within your financial means, of course.

This is true of all the objects and appliances that enter your home, down to your bed. I am always amazed how many people sleep under the worst conditions. They will say replacing their mattress is

Think in term

expensive, but all they'd have to do is not spend quite so much money going to restaurants every week. Think in terms of priority. Bed is where we spend at least one third of our lives. Think about where else you spend time and what sorts of objects and appliances surround you. Could you make your life any easier, more fulfilling, more beautiful?

Take a moment to think about your furniture, your books, your knickknacks, memorabilia, paraphernalia, all the things that gather in our home and pile up without meaning, without use, or without need. Try making a list accounting for how much time you spend where and with what. Place rooms, furnishings, and objects in order from the most time you spend to the least. Account for all your various activities and see if there are any products that could improve your life—whether it's your tennis game, your desire to cook, or the cold tiles you step on every morning. See if there isn't something you can change (or buy) that could contribute to your well-being.

I spend a great deal of time with my laptop, so I bought the best laptop I could. It's the fastest, the lightest (since I travel a lot), the most ergonomic, the simplest OS (operating system) to use, the sharpest screen, the longest battery life, and the most aesthetically pleasing. I believe that if you care about aesthetics, you care about living a seamless and perfect life. Since I look at my laptop every day and nearly all day, its beauty is very important to me.

s of priority.

There should be a profession called **REMOVERS.**

This is true of all appliances, especially stereos and televisions that take so much of our living space. Their functionality is the priority but their aesthetic appeal is a close second. Does your television have a simple, beautiful interface? Is the remote direct and easy to use? I've seen huge ones that look like they could launch spaceships but are completely incomprehensible, far from user friendly. How often have you found yourself at a friend's house unable to turn on the television out of the sheer confusion of multiple remotes for cable, DVD, VCR, and so on? It's incredibly frustrating. Once you've answered the questions of functionality and accessibility, ask yourself if it is a beautiful object, considering that it is displayed in your home—and usually occupies a significant amount of space, if not the center of your living room. Does it have the material presence, quality, form, color, and design that is beautiful, contemporary, and relevant to your life?

Now that you've had a look around your home for the most

important appliances, try to identify the opposite. The irrelevant, obsolete, clumsy, or superfluous. When was the last time you took a good look at the things in your home? How many kettles do you really need? Why is your coat closet full of things people forgot there years ago? Do you have a pile of clothes that need mending or alterations? Are you ever going to make them or would you be better off giving up and moving on? Think about anything you have multiples of. Some will make sense as replacements or backups (you can justify having two umbrellas but not six of them), while others will rise to the surface as completely superfluous, time- and energy-consuming excess. Again, anything you have been given that you do not love or want must go. You don't need to throw it in the garbage, just pass it on to someone who will appreciate it more than you (and beware when someone else tries to give you something for the same reason—they're trying to clean up their own closet!). I don't entirely believe that one man's garbage is another man's treasure: sometimes garbage is just garbage.

In general, see if you could replace any number of objects with one better multifunctional one. For example, there is no need for a different set of speakers for your television, computer, stereo, and mp3 player (unless you travel with them). You do not need a PDA (personal digital assistant), laptop, CD player, cassette player, mp3 player, DVD player, answering machine, cell phone, voice mail, and home computer. Decide on a single medium and own no more than one. The same goes for the kitchen. Do you have bowls in all sorts of mismatched shapes and sizes? Wouldn't you be better served by a set of nesting bowls that fit perfectly into one another and occupy the space of a single bowl instead of five?

Think of the resulting space
and peace of mind.

How many wires are creeping around your apartment that could be cleaned up? Are your files overstuffed with paperwork that is more than five years old? Is your closet crammed with clothes that don't fit, for when you're thinner or fatter, in case they come back in style, or because your grandmother gave them to you? The rule of thumb is that if you haven't worn them in more than a year, you can live without them.

In addition to movers, there should be a profession called *removers*. This would be especially beneficial because it's a job more easily done by someone on the outside, with no emotional attachment to the objects in question and none of that paralyzing sense of "If I've kept it this long, I may as well hold on to it for another ten years." Their job would be to drill you about everything you own: When did you last wear this sweater? Why do you still have that clunky picture frame? They would force you to look at everything and make you get rid of the things you simply don't need. Additionally, they may also reason with you: "Should bell-bottoms and platform shoes ever come back, surely you can buy another pair and free the real estate until then." If you think of it in terms of precious time and space wasted, you will find removing a lot easier.

Once you have successfully answered all these questions, do the following:

If someone you know would like it, give it away.
If it can be of use to the needy, get it to them quickly.
If it's too valuable to dispose of, put it on eBay.

Whatever you do, do *not* talk yourself into keeping it if it isn't beautiful, practical, and efficient. Only if there is a very legitimate reason for it should you ever put anything in storage. If you can store it out of the way, chances are you don't need it. I saw a sign on the door of a storage place that read "If it's worth storing, it's worth insuring." Think about that: the expense of storage and insurance, the possibility that you'll leave that stuff there for years and, yes, quite possibly decide to get rid of it then. If it's not worth insuring, it's definitely not worth storing!

If you are going to buy a second or bigger house or you have another good reason to store furniture and other objects, think carefully, pack things well so they don't get too dusty, and keep a list of what you've put away so as to avoid forgetting it, buying it again, or worse

If it's not worth insuring, it's

yet, spending hours on end looking for something that isn't there.

In New York, we all live in relatively small spaces, so often we do have things in storage, even just seasonally. Efficient as this system is, it allows us to accumulate unnecessary amounts of junk. If you have the luxury of a basement, a garage, attic, or spare bedroom, do not let it become a pack rat's paradise. Think about the day you will have to wade through there to get to what really counts: How will you get everything else out of the way?

Especially helpful in throwing or giving things away is knowing where to take them. Generally speaking, it is best to give things locally to your church or the Salvation Army or another nonprofit thrift store. If you live in New York, Housing Works will pick up your furniture by appointment and reimburse you up to $10 for a cab taken there to bring large quantities of clothes. There are also countless resources on the Web.

On that note, while I have advised that you eliminate old computers, I know that it can seem wasteful to put them out with the trash. Of course, they, too, can be recycled and, if in good condition, even donated to a good cause. You can either recycle unwanted computers, monitors, and printers though manufacturer-sponsored programs;

definitely not worth storing!

donate them to a charitable organization (in New York City, see www.nyc.gov/nycwasteless); list them with online materials-exchange services (such as www.Craigslist.org or www.Freecycle.org); or find out about electronics recycling events (e.g., www.nyc.gov/sanitation).

Furthermore, while I have yet to meet a professional "remover," there are organizing services and consultants that will come to your house and help you assess your particular situation and, better yet, aid you in organizing your home or office in such a way that you get into better habits and are able to maintain the order achieved in the future.

ADDITION BY

SUBTRACTION

ADDITION BY SUBTRACTION 101

The following are some ways to have more with less:

Streamline your possessions.

Analyze each object in your home and ask yourself the key questions: when was the last time I used it? Why do I have it? Do I need it? Does it bring meaning, memory, love, function, experience, pleasure, humor, or energy to my life?

Every decorative artifact you own should have meaning in your life:

an important memory, a religious or iconoclastic reference. If not, discard it.

Have less but better furniture

in your domestic environment. Minimize the number of objects in your kitchen—best quality, least quantity.

Clean your house for ten minutes a day

and it will always be clean.

Live with a real reflection of yourself.

Remove anything that doesn't add to your experience.

For everything you buy, give one thing away;

that way, your life maintains its equilibrium. For every gift you are given, try to dispose of the same or similar object.

Downsize your technology.

Own only one television.

Objects that are discarded should not be thrown away

but taken to a secondhand shop, given to someone else, or recycled when possible.

Wait, save, and then buy the best.

Hold out for the thing you love the most.

Have less but make it do more.

Balance and

DIET

Like good design, physical health depends on balance and (pro)portion. We've all heard of a balanced diet. We are all familiar with the food pyramid with a lot of fresh fruits and vegetables at the bottom and a lot less of what we love to eat at the apex, but we also need to find balance in how we approach what we eat and how and when we eat it.

Occasionally, you may have no choice but to eat lunch in a hurry or do something else you know is not ideal, but the key is to do everything in moderation. Don't torture yourself about what you did in the past or feel guilty about extra calories (unless it's going to make you go for a run, it's a waste of time and energy). Do think about what you're taking in, why, how, and even where. Address your issues.

Are you eating a donut for breakfast because you don't have time to boil an egg in the morning? Do you eat chips just because they're there? Could you cut down on your sugar intake without even noticing?

You can do wonders by simply being more vigilant, attentive, and attuned. Just as I observe people and they way they behave (sit, stand, eat, talk, shop, etc.), you have to learn to analyze your own behavior, to spot and know your patterns. If you are not a morning person, make sure your house is stocked with healthy snacks you can grab in the morning while your eyes are still half closed (or set your alarm fifteen minutes earlier).

(pro)portion.

Eat

don't diet.

LOOK at how we eat:

If you are tempted by snacks, catch yourself before you reach—do you really even want those peanuts, chips, or pretzels? I'm not going to tell you not to touch sugar, but make sure you enjoy it when you do! Sugar is hidden in many foods you wouldn't imagine (bread, cereal, juice) and, in particular, the "low-fat" and "fat-free" varieties of anything from yogurt to brownies. The diet industry has become a multibillion-dollar business, and it's not always in the public's best interest.

In fact, those very surreptitiously added sugars might even explain the crusade against sugar in recent years. The doctrine of "no fat" (more sugar) gave way to the Atkins era of "no carbs (sugars)" and all the fat you can eat. Is there not something inherently wrong with both of these pictures? I'd like to call for moderation and self-control, not more slogans. How about some fats and a little sugar? Or a glass of red wine?

Eat, don't diet. In my opinion, diets don't work. They are rarely balanced and are quick fixes rather than long-term solutions you can learn to live with. Forget Atkins, forget South Beach, raw food diets, juice diets, starvation, and fasting. Forget all these trends, and, most important, forget diet pills. These are extreme measures and not lasting solutions. Without strong mental discipline you will eventually return to old eating habits and regain the weight quickly. They are not natural and will certainly disrupt the balance of your system. The only thing that works for me is common sense, coupled with a genuine

while walking, working, talking, and driving.

desire to get healthy and a good dose of self-discipline. Remember that you are in control.

Don't panic (that will backfire immediately). Set reasonable objectives for yourself. Take it one step at a time. The easiest goals to lose sight of are unreasonable ones, so think before you deny yourself something, consider your circumstances, and be realistic. No need to refuse to go out for dinner, just ask for a small portion or limit yourself to one course. Simply avoid bread and picking at dessert and you'll see the difference it makes.

Whatever you do, don't wait for bad news about your health or weight to think about what you're eating today. Again, don't be fooled by the latest trends; go with the tried-and-true formula, balanced meals, lots of fruits and vegetables, and fewer trans fats and refined sugars. Preservatives seem downright dangerous, and other complicated ingredients are probably no better. Think preventively, not symptomatically.

When I arrived from Canada twelve years ago, I weighed a slender 185 pounds and exercised roughly three days a week. After living in the United States for ten years I weighed 235 pounds, even though I was still exercising and thought I was eating normally. I wasn't sure how the weight crept up on me, but now I know there were several reasons.

It has been proven that we do not gain pounds with age but that we put on weight as a result of inactivity. A **sedative/sedentary** lifestyle—sitting at computers, traveling on planes, driving our cars everywhere—is most conducive to weight gain. (I'll come back to the importance of exercise in the next chapter.)

Food is so abundant and restaurant portions are so enormous that we tend to eat far more than we need. Because of the plethora of media about food, images, places to eat everywhere, and very inexpensive food, we have indulged in this decadent lifestyle. Portions are the single biggest reason that a record number of Americans are overweight. Most restaurants serve huge portions, and once they're in front of you, you will be tempted to eat every last bite. Once your stomach is enlarged, it will take more to make you feel full. It is a vicious cycle.

Fast food is too easy, too accessible, affordable, instant, and seductive. Fast food is especially dangerous. It doesn't taste all that good, but there's something almost addictive about it—maybe

restaurant portions are so

enor

because you never feel satisfied. If you haven't seen the documentary *Supersize Me*, rent it. It will show you.

I used to eat fast food occasionally. It was convenient and provided what seemed like instant gratification. Sugar and fat are most addictive. A Big Mac without cheese has almost 600 calories, and close to half of those are from fat. The salad is no better, with hundreds of calories in the dressing alone. I never eat fast food anymore. The last time I stepped into a McDonald's was about seventeen years ago, but this alone doesn't guarantee I won't gain weight. Nor is McDonald's the culprit: We are. We have choices, now more than ever in history.

The first step to good health is to consider the quality and amount of food you're eating. If you look at Europeans as a whole, you'll see that they are nowhere near as overweight as we are. (However, with American fast-food franchises popping up on street corners from Paris to Budapest, this may soon change.) Generally speaking, most Europeans are considerably thinner than we are.

One of the principal reasons for this is the size of their portions.

MODERATION

In Europe, and even in Asia, portions are almost one third smaller than they are here. If you ate 30 percent less, either by cooking less or by leaving a third of what's on your plate, you would lose weight very rapidly. You might lose five pounds a month, and you could do it almost effortlessly. Though it may be difficult at first, you can do it gradually and adjust to this change fairly easily. Most important, you would still be able to eat most of your favorite foods.

I was brought up in a home where we were encouraged (if not forced) to finish everything on our plates, so I was accustomed to doing that, and, with the large portions, I ended up gaining a ton of weight.

Proper meals

It was a lifelong habit but I was able to break it, and you can do it too. Initially, I left only a little on the plate, maybe 10 percent. A week later, I was up to 15, then 20 percent of the meal. By the end of that first month, a third of it remained on my plate, untouched, and I wasn't even tempted by it. I had lost five pounds in those first four weeks. I felt so much better about myself that I needed no further incentive to stick to my plan.

Downsizing what you eat is not as hard as it seems—it's simply a matter of adjustment. Eating slowly, preferably sitting at a table (not walking or working on your computer), even talking with friends during meals can make a huge difference. The more calm and relaxed you are, the better. It is no surprise that people suffer from indigestion and that our drugstores are filled to the brim with antacids. Look at how we eat: while walking, working, talking, and driving. Next time, make a lunch or dinner date and converse! I always think of Monty Python's hilarious skit where couples in a restaurant are approached by waiters bearing giant topic cards to stimulate conversation. Eating should be a social experience.

Having proper meals three times a day is also a very good idea. It will keep you from snacking between meals,

times a day.

and if you take the time to sit down (yes, this is very important, on a good chair with a clean, clear table) and eat good food in a relaxed atmosphere, you will feel the results in no time. Another habit we can learn from our friends in Europe is that they are rigorous about their three meals a day. They eat light breakfasts, large lunches, and lighter dinners.

That said, they also eat all of the foods we are constantly told to avoid: high-fat cheeses, chocolate, croissants, cream sauces, and pasta. They just don't overeat. That's, again, why moderation is imperative. It means not only that you eat less and get into better habits but also that you won't be obsessing about that thing you're trying so hard to avoid. Nothing makes you crave a certain "forbidden" food more than deciding to stop eating it altogether. Again, set reasonable goals.

When I travel, I notice that most people love their sweets. A little sweet is a nice way to finish a meal, but the operative word is *little*. Remember, quality over quantity. Common sense and moderation is the best diet in the world. As we have said, in Europe, desserts are literally half the size of ours. Sweetness after dinner makes total sense to complete the palate's experience, but, like everything else we take in, we have to keep our quantities within reason. There the croissants are smaller, the cheese plates are smaller, and you get one scoop of ice cream, not four. Everything is smaller but of higher quality. Somehow we have become known the world over for the opposite: more food and less quality.

My father always said that moderation comes from mental discipline. It is about knowing how to gain more pleasure out of things when you have less of them. It is about savoring a moment's taste, smell, and experience.

Think before you eat. I won't suggest that you cut out all carbs or drink a gallon of water before every meal, but do use your common sense. For example, know what you should avoid: fast food, processed foods, and most especially, candy bars in disguise (so-called "healthy" snack bars that are full of sugar and have many more calories than you would ever imagine). If you're watching your weight, watch out for them.

Things to keep in check: Sugar is amazing, but have it in special treats and desserts, not in your cereal, your food, your meats, poultry, etc. Save it for really high-quality treats. My favorite is 70% cocoa dark chocolate by Lindt of Switzerland. This chocolate is pure and it's good for you. But remember moderation. The other way to have sugar is pure honey or maple syrup. Drink sodas that contain either cane sugar or are fruit juice sweetened, but stay away from high-fructose corn syrup. If you do indulge in a donut or cookie, try to eat it in combination with nonsweetened food or drinks, even milk, which is filling and a perfect complement. If you take sugar in your coffee, try having less or substituting it with honey. **Share desserts with others.**

In Europe, the food industry shies away from genetically modified foods and from pesticides, because that's what the population demands. Europeans seem to be more careful about what they put into their bodies, and we would do well to learn this from them, too. **Always look for quality food,** even if you have to pay a little more. It's worth it—your body is your temple. In Europe, even the simplest foods

Think
before you eat.

seem to be made with the best, purest ingredients. A box of Danish butter cookies is made with butter, flour, salt, and two or three other natural ingredients. A box of American cookies, on the other hand, begins with the same basic ingredients, then piles on the junk. Read the label. Stay away from junk.

My father was a worldly, cosmopolitan man, but when we moved to Canada he picked up many of the local habits: large portions, mediocre food, convenience. At the age of forty-nine, he had a heart attack and literally died for two minutes. He spent six months in a Toronto hospital, and when he emerged he had become another person. He had gone from a vibrant, healthy, energetic man to an old one with snow-white hair and a walker.

In the weeks ahead, he realized he had two choices. He could take care of himself, or he might die. He decided to be more careful about what he put into his body, and he approached every meal with his eyes open. Suddenly, he was paying attention to food. He needed fuel, as he always had, but from that day forward he decided he would use only premium fuel.

He ate well without going on a diet. He got back into shape. His strength returned. Over time, he weaned himself off his medication: He went from twenty-eight pills a day to one pill—a multivitamin. He did not become homeopathic. He was not into macrobiotics. He did not become a zealot. He realized that food was not the enemy, as long as he made his choices wisely,

Stay away from JUNK.

Read the label.

and for the rest of his life he enjoyed good health, energy, and a radiance most of us lose early on.

My father's heart attack changed his life for the better. I'd like to say I learned from it, but we humans are strange. We're smart enough to know that we're doing ourselves harm (food, drugs, alcohol, etc.) but it generally takes a major shock to force us to change.

I had my first shock when I moved to New York from Rhode Island. I ate out three times a day, rushing to and from my job, and going from one interview to another to try to find work. Within two months I had managed to lose thirty pounds, and I was suffering from a chronic sore throat. The doctors didn't know what was wrong with me until one of them finally suggested I get tested for food allergies. I found out I was allergic to eighteen different foods, from tomatoes to beer, and that I had damaged my immune system by ignoring what I was taking in.

I was put on a rigorous, fresh food diet. Fresh meat, fresh fish, fresh vegetables, brown rice, grains. I started the day with a light breakfast—cereal, fiber, fruit—and made lunch my principal meal. In the evening, I would eat a salad, maybe a little cottage cheese, and I'd allow myself one (natural) cookie before bed.

Initially, it was a little hard to get used to, but as my health improved it gave me the incentive to keep going. And the approach to food made sense: a small, nourishing breakfast, a pleasantly fulfilling lunch, a light dinner. I slept better. I realized there was no logic to filling my belly before bed, since the last thing I needed for sleep was all that extra fuel and calories not being burned.

It was sweets I found hardest to give up. I have a terrible sweet tooth, and I know this is my Achilles heel, but at the time I also knew I had to give them up to get better. So I did it. I redesigned my thinking because the rewards were worth it. Of course, before long, I was busy again and the old habits took over: food on the run, sodas, restaurants, large portions, pizza, and ice cream.

Then, during the Milan furniture fair, I did a short video clip for Italian MTV where I was asked to strip down to my underwear in quick frame to demonstrate a line of furniture I designed that could be stripped down. I saw myself that night on television in a hotel room and realized I was destined for health problems with my excessive weight (especially around the middle, which is a warning for heart disease, diabetes, and related problems).

That was my second big shock: I was getting fat. I wasn't looking my best and this was a shock to my ego, too, so I decided I had to do something about it. I got back to New York and took action. I ended up losing fifty pounds in five months.

One day I was in a great Italian restaurant, one of those places where you can see the kitchen from your table, and I watched the sous-chef put half a stick of butter into my pasta. Suddenly, it struck me: No wonder it tastes so good! I realized that all that goodness could kill me, as it had almost killed my father, and right there and then I made a life-changing decision. I was going to learn how to cook. If I cooked, I'd be able to control exactly what I put into my body.

And I would be sure to lose weight. I was right on both counts, and cooking turned out to be a lot of fun, relaxing, and, yes, very creative.

Cooking is a very creative and rewarding endeavor. First of all, you have to know where to shop and allow yourself to be inspired. Don't go to the market with preconceived notions, but see what's out there, what's in season, what looks good, and, above all, what looks new and fresh. There are plenty of books and websites you can consult, and once you've learned the basics you can experiment even with the most unusual ingredients. Leave the recipes behind and let your imagination run wild. Don't be intimidated by exotic ingredients or things you've never made before. We are lucky to have so many options that we should never be bored by what we eat. So, scout out some good shops, both general interest and specialty stores. Locate the best greengrocers, fishmongers, butchers, and bakers. If you have a farmer's market on certain days of the week, make a point of going

Allow yourself to be inspired.

there—put it on your calendar if you have to. And who better to get cooking tips from than the growers themselves!

When shopping, remember not to deprive yourself. Snacking between meals is fine, as long as you watch what you eat. Always think before you put anything into your mouth. Keep healthy food around the house for lunch and the occasional snack. Mixed nuts, beans, organic freeze-dried soups (just add water), and good cheeses—a simple Jarlsberg or a nice Gouda. I'm also a fan of brown and wild rice, and I keep plenty of organic, high-fiber cereals on hand. Make sure the cereals are sugarless. Most cereals are loaded with corn syrup and sugar, but they manage to create the illusion that they're full of good things. Read the ingredients. Sometimes you can find the healthy cereals right next to the bad ones, if you look for them. Again, I want to stress that you don't have to hunt for any of these products in a fancy gourmet shop. They are available in most of the national, mass-market grocery stores.

And, while on the subject of grocery stores, I'd like to address the importance of buying food and water that has traveled the least distance possible. Don't ignore the healthy things that exist in your own backyard. If you can get good grapes from your own community, why buy those that are imported from Chile? There's nothing wrong with them, but you are always better off consuming foodstuffs grown closer to home. There's something spiritually coherent about it: Eat what's there. Eat what's in season. It's so much better for you.

A related concern of mine is water. I don't understand the national craze with bottled water. The local water is usually very good and has the added benefit of containing fluoride. In a blind taste test, New York city tap water fared no worse than the bottled brands and, most

Cooking =

important, scientists found that there was no greater likelihood of being exposed to *E. coli* and other bacteria from tap water. But most of us go for the bottled brands, and the more exotic sounding the better. What does it mean when you're told that a certain brand came from a virgin spring, high in the French Alps? Think about it. To me, it means that the water had to be shipped over great distances, and that in the process it has added more pollution to the environment than you can imagine, and that you are doing a disservice to humanity by buying it. Learn to love your own spring or even tap water.

Now back to the kitchen. Remember, cooking is a lot like therapy. Don't let it stress you out. If you're a novice, start cooking for yourself and, as you develop confidence, invite friends—first the ones who don't know how to cook (they're always very appreciative) and then work your way to the ones who do.

At the end of the day or on a weekend it can be a very relaxing thing to do. You are focused on the task at hand, so the other issues in your life disappear into the background. You go to the grocery store or local farmer's market, pick up what you need (this, too, should be an aesthetic experience), then bring it home and wash, chop, sizzle, and grill. It's a real stress reliever—you and your cookbook and your nice pans and everything happening exactly the way you decide it's going

therapy.

to happen. When dinner is done and you're sitting in front of it, you feel a tremendous sense of accomplishment. It really is a wonderful way to end the day or week. In fact, you may want to consider making extra portions to store or freeze for the week ahead. And if you put them in smaller Tupperware containers you can be assured that you'll eat no more than a single portion at a time!

I can't say that my wife and I cook every day; we don't. Both of us are busy people, and sometimes it's much easier to go out to a local restaurant or to order in. But, to this day, when I'm not traveling, I make an effort to cook at least three or four nights a week. I not only enjoy it but it keeps me healthy. I love knowing what I'm eating and I

simple meals, PURE

natural INGREDIENTS.

love transforming all the disparate ingredients into a meal. Even in the best restaurants, you never know exactly what they are putting into your food. But when you eat at home, you are directing the show to your particular specifications.

I always opt for simple meals, with pure, natural ingredients. If I want pheasant under glass, I'll go to a restaurant. But at home, it's best to avoid complicated pyrotechnics. We should look for fresh, organic vegetables, free-range chicken, and beef that hasn't been fed any chemicals. And it's easy to find these items. Almost every grocery store in America is devoting more and more space to health-conscious consumers, because at long last we've begun to demand it. And it's such a pleasure to make a salad at home that beats the one you get at the local restaurant.

For example, you can buy:

Organic greens (even prewashed)	Organic carrots
Red onion	Organic cherry tomatoes
String beans	Red and green peppers
Fresh black olives	A can of solid white tuna
Organic mushrooms (chanterelle are my favorites)	

Mix it up with pure, cold-pressed olive oil and a little balsamic vinegar, add a hardboiled egg, and voilà! It's a classic Niçoise salad, an amazing meal in five minutes.

Pasta is also fast, simple, and versatile, with countless recipes for you to try. And, despite what the anticarb zealots have to say, it's good for you, particularly when you cook it al dente. Just remember to keep the portions small, and do not overcook or overdress.

My favorite simple pasta dish is penne with shrimp cooked al dente. I used to make it with with hot turkey sausage Bolognese sauce, but now I'm a pescetarian. It is simple (the recipe is below) and the pasta takes only ten minutes to cook. A good bottle of red wine and you're all set. The best reds are Italian (Barolo, Amarone, Barbera d'Asti), but Chilean, Argentinian, Portuguese, and Spanish are just as good and really inexpensive. Here's the recipe:

PASTA WITH SHRIMP, TOMATOES, AND ARUGULA

12 ounces penne (whole wheat organic)

3 tablespoons olive oil (preferably extra-virgin)

8 ounces uncooked large shrimp, peeled, cleaned, coarsely chopped

2 tablespoons chopped fresh basil

2 garlic cloves, pressed

1 pound tomatoes, cored, cut into wedges

3 bunches arugula, stems trimmed

Cook pasta in a large pot of boiling salted water until tender but still firm. In the meantime, heat oil in large nonstick skillet over medium heat. Add shrimp, basil, and garlic. Stir until shrimp are almost cooked through, about 3 minutes. Add tomatoes and stir 2 minutes. Ladle out ½ cup pasta cooking liquid and reserve. Drain pasta. Add pasta, arugula, and reserved ½ cup pasta cooking liquid to skillet and toss until heated through, about 3 minutes. Season with salt and pepper.

On weekends, I love making **KARTINIs** and relaxing by the pool of my country house. Here's my mix:

3 parts freezing Bombay Sapphire gin

1 part Martini Rossi white vermouth

1 part Campari

1 slice of watermelon

Raspberries

Lemon

1. Fill a Karim glass martini shaker about $3/4$ with cracked ice.
2. Pour gin, vermouth, and Campari into the shaker and let stand for sixty seconds.
3. Shake, shake, shake with vigor, diagonally.
4. Put that shaker down and get two well chilled karimartini glasses from the freezer.
5. Each glass gets a twist, a watermelon slice, and some raspberries.
6. Strain your chilly gin into each glass.
7. Sip and kick back with a book on Hume, Heidegger, or Sartre.

Another crucial advantage of home cooking is the multidimensional aesthetic experience. Eating, like so many other activities we do without thinking or realizing, should be an aesthetic experience. Try to make the meal as beautiful as possible. Set the table with care. Use beautiful plates and flatware, napkins in different colors. Have flowers. Use bowls that will complement their contents, place food with care and make sure that the lighting, music, and atmosphere are the best they can be.

Think

Your body is

Don't

Common sense

Be an educated

Quality

Eat

Set

Sit

before you eat.

your temple.

starve.

+ moderation.

consumer.

vs. Quantity.

locally.

the table.

down. **Converse.**

FITNESS

Learn to look, feel, and live younger.

Six months after seeing myself on Italian television, I was transformed. I was in good shape and felt better than ever, physically and mentally. As much as I've never been one to exercise for fun, I can't stress enough how important it is for your mind, as well as your body. When I'm exercising regularly, I see and think more clearly, I'm sharp and attuned. I feel so much better and so much stronger, ready to face anything, I'm mentally, physically, and psychologically stronger. It can be a real transformation from the inside out. In a sense it was a big problem solved—not in the moment but for the long haul.

I had to work out to get back into shape, and it wasn't easy. I have a deep admiration for people who stay fit because I know what it takes. It doesn't always come naturally and, if you don't love it, it's really hard to make the time. If you live in a big city, chances are you have too much to do all the time, places to go in the evenings, work to get to in the mornings, and weekends filled with everything you do not get to beforehand. Lunch is barely a break. Going to the gym, pool, or even yoga means packing a lot of stuff and possibly carrying it around all day and then out for dinner. In the city, there's no room to run and the air is not so good. We're all in the same boat, but a lot of these are excuses.

Once you're out there, it's really not that bad. In fact, it becomes easier, even pleasurable.

For me, getting in shape was well worth it. Staying in shape is even better. At the time, I joined a local gym and developed some great habits; now I run six miles a day and I continue to enjoy it.

Exercise does not have to be difficult or time consuming. It can be quite simple, in fact. Half the battle is getting on with it. If you're out of shape, a brisk walk three times a week is a good start. After a week, you can walk a little further and bit faster. After another, you might find you want to try speed walking, then jogging. Eventually, you might find that you like running. And even if you don't, a good walk is a great thing. It gets you out, breathing fresh air, looking around, being inspired, and leaving tensions behind.

If you need a break, and you'd rather tune out, bring your mp3 player. Download your favorite music or, better yet, some new music. Make a point of asking friends and family for their favorites and start an exchange. Speaking of which, there are probably a few calls you could make while you're on your daily walk: your mother, your uncle, your sister, or the college friend you haven't spoken to in years. Think of it as a time to catch up.

If you don't like to exercise per se, don't think of it as an end in itself,

cuses

but work it into your daily routine. Instead of driving for fifteen minutes, walk. Do some stretching while you watch TV. Talk a friend into taking up squash or tennis. Play soccer or basketball on the weekends. Take a walk in the park or ride your bike along the river. If you don't have a dog, volunteer to take your neighbor's for a walk—you'll be doing them and yourself a favor. Go swimming whenever you can, it's hydromassage and exercise in one.

Don't expect the impossible. Change takes time. Start with reasonable goals and take it one step, one lap, one jog at a time. Design a plan that works for you. Make yourself a schedule to ensure that you find the time, and be ready with everything you need when the time comes. Make it fun. Kudos every time you get out. Be proud of yourself for even making the effort. Once your routine is set in motion, you will be grateful. You will feel results before you begin to see them. Once you see them, you'll be encouraged to stay on track and every day will be easier.

Make it fun!

If it's incentive you need . . .

1. **Try great music.** Music makes you move. Go for it. Be your own DJ. Make playlists for different workouts, moods, and places. Here's one of mine:

DISCO ROCKS

Roxy Music: "Lover"

Hall & Oates: "One on One"

Paul McCartney: "Goodnight Tonight"

Alan Parsons Project: "Voyager"

Boz Scaggs: "Lowdown"

Fleetwood Mac: "Tusk"

Toto: "Georgy Porgy"

Rolling Stones: "Miss You"

Kinks: "(Wish I Could Fly) Like Superman"

Rod Stewart: "Do You Think I'm Sexy?"

Stranglers: "Skin Deep"

Queen: "Body Language"

Alan Parsons Project: "I Wouldn't Want to Be Like You"

Steve Miller: "Macho City"

The Tubes: "Slipped My Disco"

Sparks: "Number One Song in Heaven"

David Bowie: "Loving the Alien"

Steely Dan: "Gaucho"

The Tubes: "Prime Time"

Hall & Oates: "I Can't Go For That (No Can Do)"

Giorgio Moroder: "Knights in White Satin"

Sparks: "With All My Might"

Queen: "Another One Bites the Dust"

Roxy Music: "Dance Away"

Frank Zappa: "Disco Boy"

Pink Floyd: "Run Like Hell"

Sweet: "Love Is Like Oxygen"

Be-Bop Deluxe: "Electrical Language"

Ultravox: "Quiet Man"

David Bowie: "John, I'm Only Dancing"

The Doobie Brothers: "What a Fool Believes"

Fleetwood Mac: "Looking Out for Love"

Sparks: "When I Am With You"

Steely Dan: "Do It Again" (Club Mix)

Kiss: "I Was Made for Loving You Baby"

2. If your local pool has a sauna, make time to go there after your swim. That's an especially good motivator on cold winter days.
3. Make a point of getting a great fruit juice or smoothie on your way to the gym.
4. Work out with your partner. Make plans to meet a friend.
5. Don't sit at the movies eating popcorn; take your friend on a long walk and talk.

Whatever you decide to do, whether it's weight lifting, jogging, or tae kwon do, think of how to improve the experience:

1. **Remember what you wear.** Good, comfortable, high-tech, versatile, modern, futuristic gear can make all the difference.
2. Think of your feet. **Great sneakers are imperative.** Get the information you need. What are the best shoes for each purpose, terrain, and experience level?
3. Make sure you're warm or cool enough. **Bring layers.**
4. **Wear colors you love.** Mix them according to your mood. Make every time you head out feel new and inspiring.
5. **Travel light.** Bring the essentials, even water if you feel you need to, but stay streamlined. Carry no excess baggage. Hang or clip your keys and mp3 player. Put some cash in your shoes in case you want to stop for water, and go.

Starting is by far the hardest part. Getting out there is literally half the battle. Once you're there, with great music pumping through your system, you will wonder why it took you so long to get there. When you start getting into it, you'll be amazed how much you enjoy it and

IMPROVE
the experience.

also how much you will miss it when you can't make the time. I no longer stay in a hotel that doesn't have a gym.

You will enjoy your new, leaner, better, fitter, more streamlined body. Putting on clothes will become a pleasure. When you feel better about yourself, you reflect it, you appear more confident, and the people around you will take notice. You'll hear compliments and be inspired to go on. When you are stronger inside and out, you'll find you cope better with everyday stresses, get more done, and become more efficient in every way.

Among the many benefits of exercise, there is the fact that it makes you more attuned to your body and that's by far the best way to avert a whole plethora of problems. By knowing our bodies we can spot symptoms at the nascent stage.

If you're prone to a particular ailment, ask your doctor about preventive measures—don't procrastinate. Most of us could feel a lot better every day if we merely paid more attention to ourselves and to our bodies' needs. You may want to see a nutritionist or undergo some tests to identify allergies and intolerances. Sometimes eliminating one or two things from your diet (even ones you didn't realize you were taking in) can have immediate results.

The same can be said of exercise. The moment you get into the habit of stretching a few times a day, doing some kind of cardiovascular workout a few times a week, and gradually becoming stronger, you will notice that a lot of nagging aches and pains will cease to plague

Enjoy your NEW BODY.

you. Your neck is less likely to feel stiff from staring at the computer, and your lower back won't be quite as taxed when you're sitting at a desk all day long. When your abdominal muscles begin to hold you up a little better, your posture will improve dramatically and you may even feel that you've gained an inch or two in the process.

Your eyes need exercise, too. Look away from the computer and focus on something far away for a minute. You should also get up and walk around every twenty minutes or so; if you're likely to forget, set the alarm on your computer to remind you. In fact, you should treat your exercise routine like you would any other important commitment: mark it on your calendar; it's no less important than a business meeting or a doctor's appointment.

On that note, there are many ways to boost your immune system. Look into the appropriate foods, vitamins, herbs, and other supplements that cater to your specific needs. And no matter how good you feel, get your yearly checkups. Make sure you have a good doctor and that he or she has all your records in order, test results, etc., even those from past physicians. Let them get a well-rounded view of your salutary state.

As mentioned with regard to clutter, you should take care not to let tensions accumulate in your body. Like toxins, they will take their toll. Take care of yourself. The moment you start to feel tightness in your neck and shoulders, do some exercises. Get a massage as often as you can and enjoy it. Don't schedule it between meetings but when you know you can rest afterward. When you start to feel run down, take some vitamins, drink a lot of water, stay warm, and get a good night's sleep. I know it sounds obvious, but *do you do it?*

Exercise is about redesigning your body from the inside out. Good health is about achieving efficiency, the perfect marriage of form and function, and becoming your own best design.

Love

- Social Life
- Beauty
- Fashion
- Sex
- Death

Each individual is an extension of

the **human race.**

Each person has significance.

SOCIAL LIFE

To have family and friends is a fundamental part of the human experience. To love and respect others is the single most important message we receive from all religions throughout time and across all physical boundaries. Each person has significance, a contribution that we must respect. Each individual is an extension of the human race.

Is conflict inevitable? Is it natural for humans to hate, to be violent, to have greed, to be selfish, to be racist, to be gluttonous? This is an ongoing anthropological and ontological discussion. Some say it's inevitable, but I don't subscribe to that theory. I think that the violence, hatred, and jealously are all behavioral and that we can have perfect harmony, romance, and a peaceful world if we are brought up with and surrounded by nothing else. Many cultures are very peaceful, considerate, and respectful of others—as well as the environment. It is not impossible. It is what we must strive for. Love and friendship give meaning to our existence.

We shape and design our own world, and, generally speaking, the way we are treated depends on how we treat others. This is the basic notion underlying the theory of Karma. What we put out in the world is what will come back to us. If I'm nice and treat someone well, they will in turn pay me their respects. Try it. When I enter an elevator I find that it is common for no one to speak. I always say hello, good evening, or good night, comment on the weather or how slow the elevator is, or make a joke about vertical teleporting. I always get a polite reciprocation. Then the next time that person enters an elevator, a building, a shop, or an airplane, he or she is more likely to break the silence by greeting someone.

On a related note, I would like to point out that humor is another very important factor of the human condition. I think that everything should be smart and beautiful and holistically designed, experiential and ecological, but also that every aspect of our lives should be injected with the spirit of humor, because it lightens up this overly serious thing we call life. I say this now because I think it's important in the context of friendship. It can create an instant bond with the person next to you in the elevator. But you will need a good dose of it to get though life—in relationships of love and with family especially!

Socializing should be a **positive** experience.

Having a network of good friends is critical. It helps you stay a well-rounded person, and it can also take pressure off your mate. You can't always be everything to your partner, and you should remember that he or she cannot be everything to you either. We tend to think of happiness as a state that should last forever but, like other emotions, it has its peaks and valleys. In Western society, we rely very heavily on a partner for love, intimacy, and support, sometimes to the point of codependence. Ideally, we should be able to stand alone and complement—not complete—each other. Just as we have said that we should set realistic expectations for ourselves, we should do the same for others. If you expect too much from people, you will not only be disappointed, you will also be at fault.

Your social life is important and it too can be redesigned to get the most out of it.

ON FRIENDS

Let's discuss friends. You can't be too demanding of friends. You must accept friends for who they are, their good and their bad, their traits, their habits, their values, whether you believe in them or not, and so on. If you really have trouble with them, then you should just not waste your time. If there is no compatibility there, it's not a friendship. True friendship is about respect, not about having a clone of yourself. I used to always find fault with my friends. After a dinner I would complain about something they said or be critical about what they were doing with their lives. Then I realized over time that I must have somehow sent these messages to them, because they would eventually stop calling and I would find myself friendless. I realized that if I had negative things to say about them, then I didn't really treasure or cherish the friendship.

Think about your friends. Why are they your friends? The world would be a more honest place if you saw only the friends you really wanted to see—the friends you truly care about. Try not to socialize for the sake of doing something or just for company.

Reduce
commitments.

Socializing should be a positive experience: to learn, to enjoy, to engage, to communicate, not just a way to get out of the house. Experience is the most important part of living: Human contact and the exchange of ideas is what life is all about. You can redesign your social life. You can see only those people you find truly worthwhile.

I know this will sound harsh, but you should learn to edit your social obligations, even friends and acquaintances. When I say "friends" here, I mean it in the broadest sense: all the people you see, know from work, friends of friends you have little in common with, and any others you feel an obligation to see. If you moved away and were back in town for a week, who would you really want to see? Who would you make real time for? Start there.

Once you've settled on your true friends—those that support, nurture, entertain, and teach—you can focus on reciprocating and being the best friend you can. Maybe you couldn't be a best friend to everyone, or game for every outing, but when you narrow it down to your nearest and dearest, then you can focus on being all that you can to them. Good friendships are nourishing and stimulating.

Spread the wealth.

Keep your word. Do what you say you're going to do.

Be on time. If you can be on time for therapy, or to drop your kids off at school, why can't you be on time for lunch with a friend?

Return phone calls, e-mails, and letters within twenty-four hours of receiving them, even if it's just to say a quick "hello" so that the other person will know you're thinking of them.

Redesign the way you meet people. People say they never meet anyone new, but that's a lousy excuse. You have to reach out.

Throw a party. Join a group.
Visit a museum. Make friends online.

Try to have a dinner party once a month. Find six people you want to be with for one evening, ask new friends you've just met, or, better yet, invite three people you like and ask each of them to bring a friend you don't know. Dinner parties are a lot of fun. They will make your life richer, more exciting. Make it a potluck in terms of people and food. Then there's less pressure on the host and a better chance to encounter something—or someone—new. You can even spark some healthy competition if everyone is trying to cook something exotic or bring a more interesting friend.

As new people come into your life, the old ones are often replaced. Again, this sounds harsh, but many friendships are not about friendship at all, but about habit. Friendship is not just about circumventing your loneliness; it's about mutual support. Friendship is about give and take, having and providing a support structure. Friendship is about inspiring and encouraging each other.

Learn to spend time with yourself. Very few of us know how to do this or even realize how important it is. We all lead demanding lives, and often feel we barely have time for our immediate family, but we must not be afraid to seek out some time alone as that is the way we come to terms with ourselves and our present situation. From spending time alone you can come back refreshed and truly prepared to focus on others. It's a way to recharge your energies and to be the best that you can.

EXPA
YOUR WORLD.

STOP MAKING EXCUSES.

AND

ON LOVE

Regardless of culture, religion, or language, we all have similar needs, aspirations, and dreams. The collective need is love. Love is the glue that gives us civility, passion, desire, security, unconditionality, and a reason to be. Love is the thread that connects the human race.

Love is simple. It is the need to feel secure in the world, to be loved and to give love. Love tells us someone cares for us, supports us, encourages us. We are loved and in turn we feel secure. To love is to give totally to someone and make another feel loved. To receive that security is to be loved. It gives us self-assurance and self-confidence. It is a rewarding feeling of fulfilling a very primordial part of us. We are all capable of so much more when we are loved. The secret of greatness is to love and be loved.

Love is *not* the new religion. People search for salvation in love. But this is wrong. Love isn't about salvation. Many people talk about feeling "completed" in love. You see yourself reflected in the other's eyes, and you feel worthy. There is a Greek myth that we were actually hermaphroditic creatures who were cut in half by Zeus. Love, then, is the pressure to make ourselves whole again, to restore that lost unity. But that type of love is unhealthy. It means losing yourself in another person.

Love is about standing alone. A poorly designed vase would be one that rested against another and would collapse if it were moved, set aside, or forced to stand on its own. But take a look at my "kissing" salt and pepper shakers. They stand together and complement each other beautifully, but they also support themselves.

You should have the ability to stand on your own, straight and strong. **You were not designed to be supported by another.** You can complement one another, provide companionship, bring children into the world, and achieve a sense of equilibrium, but you can't hold each other up. It is too much to ask; it will drain the other person and exhaust the relationship. Before you even meet someone, you need to be that integral strong vase. If you are too much in need of repair, you will be sapping the other of their energy.

Like vases, people should be together because they work well together. I have witnessed so many relationships—relationships of love, of companionship, of business, of dependency, of familiarity—and there is one simple and obvious notion that keeps these relationships together—compatibility.

I don't agree with the saying that "opposites attract." Opposites distract. If I have a good relationship with a client, it is because my work is compatible with what they produce. We have a similar vision, similar values, and similar tastes. Likes attract. If I have a good relationship with my team in sports, it is because we are similar in vision, strategy, personalities, and goals. If I love someone and they love me, we have similar needs, desires, lifestyles, interests, values, customs, dress, and beliefs.

It's the snap and crackle of love between equals that makes love work. It's what keeps it exciting. I don't need someone to complete me or, even less, to cook me dinner. I need a partner.

Healthy relationships are about cooperating. They are not about judgment but about realizing that your partner is not perfect. He or she is human, conflicted, even confused. In a solid relationship, you accept your partner's shortcomings because they are simply part of the package. It has been said that the issue isn't the fact that there are problems but the belief that there shouldn't be any.

We all have expectations. Not all of them will be fulfilled. Disappointment is part of life. Learn to deal with it.

Sometimes, love is a struggle. You can't escape that struggle. You

OPPOSITES

DISTRACT.

move toward it and address it. **Remember that a struggle is an opportunity to grow.** Our desire to avoid struggle and pain is extremely harmful, even psychologically damaging. Running away can lead to no good.

A critical failure in relationships is forcing someone to be not who they are but an image of who you think they should be. Think about the things you're asking of that person. Could those demands really be speaking to your needs? Are you asking them to take care of your own shortcomings? Are the faults you see in others really your own? Are you asking someone to fulfill needs that might not be entirely reasonable?

I was brought up in a family in which my father, an artist and very passionate, seemed to have no boundaries. And my mother looked to him for entertainment. He had his art and it was enough for him, but she had mostly him, and they fought con-stantly. If she had found fulfillment elsewhere, they might have had a better, stronger marriage.

So I learned early that possessiveness coupled with neediness will add up to an unhappy situation.

I met my wife, Megan, twelve years ago, and in all that time we've never had an argument. Both of us are completely self-nourishing and very self-fulfilled. We are not looking for the other to fill some void. The other reason we do so well is that we both have almost exactly the same interests. I'm a designer and she's a painter, and we're both interested in our respective professions. But we're both also interested in art, architecture, film, design, and painting. Our backgrounds are somewhat different. She's from Connecticut and is part Canadian; I'm from the other side of the world and only lived in Canada, but we get along. It's almost seamless—we always have things to talk about.

Opposites don't attract.

If members of a couple are too different, they can't share their worlds. Every doctor whose wife is not a physician will have trouble communicating with her the intricacies of his work. Perhaps if his wife has her own divergent interests, it doesn't matter as long as they have something else in common and each one has someone else—a good friend or family member—to discuss work-related matters with. That wouldn't be the ideal for me, but it works for some people. My relationship with Megan is very much about togetherness, but I'm sure there are people who would be critical of that, too. Either way, the key is to be nourished by your own work, not to seek nourishment and validation in a partner, but to seek a partner in a partner.

While I can see that being with someone very different could be stimulating, I think that people who don't share interests tend to communicate less and less with time. This is especially true if you have little interest in what the other person does. If you're not interested in his or her work, you will be challenged. Like it or not, that is how they spend the majority of their time. Work is an integral part of our daily lives, and it can be a common ground, a place to meet and to connect. Of course, you can work in different worlds, but you might both like gourmet cooking or hiking. Perhaps one of these is your bond. In fact, many of my friends work in different worlds and they bring something home that is different and interesting to the other. An exchange of ideas takes place every day, and there's something to be said for that.

Good relationships require some work. In most relationships, the honeymoon ends before you know it. Before long, you get caught in the minutiae of day-to-day living. Getting to work on time. Fighting for that promotion. Having kids. Picking up the dry cleaning. Taking the car to the shop. This part of your life has to be redesigned so that it works seamlessly. There needs to be a sharing of the less pleasant responsibilities so that you feel as if you're in a true partnership.

Keep in mind that people do change. This might seem obvious, but we lose track of it. In fact, some say we don't change at all, but we do. We all go through stages: setbacks, successes, failures. Things we once cared about will lose their meaning and new things come to take their place. The things that make you happy can change from one day to the next.

Find the balance. Sometimes we get into a relationship and everyone else is shunted off into the background. We cut other people off. We make our partner take up the slack. Again, we are expecting too much of them. You know the old story about the friend who falls in

Seek a partner in a partner.

love and disappears and you never hear from him again. Then the relationship is over and he's back with his tail between his legs. The point is: Why can't people fall in love sensibly? Love isn't a destination. You don't get there and leave the rest of your world behind.

Love is highly illogical sometimes, so step back and take a deep breath. Think about who you are with, what you are doing, and why you are doing it. The idea is not to hold back, but to proceed with cautious intelligence.

Don't go into a relationship thinking you're going to fix something. In the design world, nothing is perfect, either. A relationship isn't about fixing or redesigning other people. It's about accepting them, flaws and all. How many times have you heard someone say, "Oh, she's

comm

perfect, except for the way she talks to waiters, but I can fix that"? Many people who go into relationships thinking they will redesign their mate are really struggling with their own needs. There are things in their hearts and souls that remain unresolved, many of them going back to childhood. People need to deal with their own issues, not look to be saved from them by another person.

If you have unreasonable expectations, you will be disappointed.

If I find a perfectly nice chair, how can I be disappointed that it won't work as a table? A chair is a chair is a chair. That person you're getting to know, that's who he or she is. You may discover new and exciting things about them, but don't expect to change them.

You should also bear in mind that people are sometimes afraid of change in a partner, worried that they'll become another person. Sometimes you hear of relationships in which one of the partners is deliberately holding the other back. He or she is afraid that the person might find great success and perhaps be changed by the attention—that the risk to the relationship is too much to bear. But if you really love another person, you want the best for them. If you don't, you should perhaps reexamine the relationship.

Learn to communicate. Learn to be open about your issues. You can get to know a great deal about yourself through your relationship with a loved one. When you know someone truly cares about you, they can help you change the things in yourself that need changing.

nicate

But you have to want to change them.

In my own relationship with Megan, we still do something from time to time that started very early on. We'll sit down to dinner one night and I'll say, "If there were three things you wanted to change about me, what would they be?" It opens up a dialogue. Maybe I've been self-absorbed lately, or not loving enough, or not attentive enough. I'd like to know before it's too late. We discuss these "three things," but we do it with love and kindness, and we have grown as a result, both as individuals and as a team.

Inspire each other to do greater things. Reach for the moon.

When Megan and I discuss the things we want to change, we both take the time to ask ourselves why we want to make these changes. In other words, is it her or is it me? Often, if you want to change something in the other person, it is because it speaks to your own needs and shortcomings. As we grow and evolve, we should help each other become better versions of ourselves. That said, do not rely on your partner for validation. Ask for constructive criticism and support but remember to stand on your own, like the well-designed vase.

Couples should complement—not complete—one another.

Beyond companionship, intellectual stimulation, and raising a family, one of the earmarks of a successful relationship is fighting constructively. Design your arguments well. Many times when I see people argue, I notice they are simply waiting for the other to finish so

ancing act.

they can state their case or defend themselves or whatever it is they are trying to do. They are too busy arguing to listen. This is not going to help. We have to listen to what the other is saying if we're going to make any progress. Let them state their case and take time to process the message. It will probably affect your "defense" in a more positive and proactive manner.

Love is a balancing act. The need to get close to someone can be terrifying—it is the notion of being swallowed up in a relationship. But keeping your distance when you are in love is also scary: It's nice to be connected to someone in a world that can be quite unfriendly at times. Stop thinking that love is the answer to life's problems. It isn't. It's a nice way of making your way in the world. If you expect your partner to make you happy, you're in for disappointments. Somebody once said, "Marriage is a nice place to experience happiness, but it doesn't provide happiness." We tend to think of happiness as a state that should last forever, but like other emotions it too has its peaks and valleys.

Know yourself.

Know what you want. Most people don't even know what makes them happy, and they're not prepared when that thing strikes. Assess your current situation and open yourself up to the endless possibilities.

Love is about possibilities, not answers.

1. **Put yourself in someone else's shoes.** Be nice, helpful, and supportive.

2. **Stay in touch!** Even if you are very busy, find simple ways of maintaining contact. If you do not have the time to visit often, call once a week.

3. **Always remember birthdays, anniversaries, and important dates for friends and family members.** Put these on a calendar if you can't remember them. There are even websites that will store this information for you (www.birthdayalarm.com).

4. **Make an effort to keep friends.** In this age in which work and time are so demanding, the best way to stay in touch with friends (in seconds!) are technologies such as e-mail, instant messaging, SMS, text messages, digital pictures, and so on.

5. Today, think of a friend or family member and send them a quick message. **Make them smile, laugh, think.**

6. **Challenge and share ideas:** books you've read, films you've seen, ideas you've found compelling.

7. **Go to art shows, museums, and exhibitions with friends.** Let your intellect and friendships grow simultaneously.

8. **Never be possessive or jealous.** You do not have an exclusive; you do not own your family or friends.

9. **Don't waste time with people if you have nothing in common.** There must be a nexus. Commonality engages us, feeds us, inspires us, and fulfills us.

10. **You should always be learning from relationships.** In turn, you should always be teaching, too. This is how friendships flourish and grow to have value and importance.

11. **Don't just socialize to occupy time.** It is better to be productive than to engage in vapid conversation. You will regret spending time vacuously.

12. **Spend quality time alone,** as well as with a spouse or family member.

13. **Family members are not automatically friends.** Friendship is earned by showing love, dedication, trust, and support.

14. **Surprise your friends.** Get flowers, send a card, e-mail a picture, visit, give them a kiss when you next seem them.

15. Don't just talk—*listen.*

16. If a friendship leaves you feeling empty, it was not meant to be.

17. **Blood is not thicker than water.**

18. **Families are complex entities.** You only have one and it is sacred. Always be good to everyone in your family. The demise of the family is the demise of culture.

19. **Surround yourself with positive people.** If someone is negative, make them aware of it. Friends must be very honest; this builds a bond and establishes trust.

20. **Awareness is the first step to changing and designing your social life.**

Beauty is

inextricably linked with the way you feel about and treat yourself.

How would I define beauty? Beauty would be a combination of all the performance, function, material, and form in one. To me it also means that the object is a reflection of its technology, its performance, its use, and its part of material culture. Beauty is the combination of the inside and out. Beauty is not just surface but the holistic entity of something. When we describe people as beautiful, their physical makeup and mental makeup are one. Beauty is not just skin deep. Design is not just skin deep. Design is the concept of the inner and outer combined—a holistically complete notion.

As a designer I am constantly thinking about beauty: the beauty of objects, environments, and experiences; beauty as it relates to form, function, and entertainment. Physical beauty is not easy to define; it is subjective and lies somewhere beneath the surface. There's an objective component, of course, but true beauty is intangible, it lies in a combination of thoughts, actions, spirituality, individuality, confidence, and a myriad of factors beyond definition.

Beauty is about image, but it's also an aesthetic experience. It's about finding the best elements in your own person, both external and internal, and making the most of them. In that sense, you might say that beauty is a form of self-exploitation. Beauty is inextricably linked with the way you feel about and treat yourself.

Think of it in terms of design. When I design something, I take a look at the elements that already work, I make the most of them, then try to improve on the existing system as a whole. You should think of yourself in the same way. You are a complex, designed system, an existing system, and there is always room for improvement. **The goal is not to become another person but to become the best of yourself.** Beauty is about finding your assets and making the most of them.

Too many of us address the problem from the wrong side. We take for granted what we have and focus on what we don't: Women with straight hair perm it, while the ones with curly hair iron it straight; tall men have complexes and trouble finding clothes that fit, while short ones think everything would be different if they could just grow another inch. Everyone has something that's too big, too small, or nonexistent. We all have physical flaws, but we don't need to obsess over them.

We are all better served by focusing our energy on our strengths and by focusing on the small gifts that set us apart as individuals.

If you're a woman with beautiful eyes, show them off. Exploit them. Use makeup in a way that forces people to look directly into your eyes. And hold that gaze. The philosopher Martin Buber said that looking into another persons eyes could have the intensity of a religious experience. Keep that in mind; make that your goal.

Thick brows are beautiful. If you have thick brows, use an eyebrow pencil and exaggerate them. Anyone can have thin brows, but thick brows you can't fake.

If you have dark hair, make it even darker. If you are a brunette, be a brunette. Don't try to be a blonde. If you have curly hair, make it even more wildly curly, and if your hair is ramrod straight, let it fall.

Exaggerate your assets.

In design, I have a similar approach. I work with what I'm given, and I try to make it honest in both form and function. I'll give you an example of something that fails miserably at this: the stereo. Electronic components have become

Exagg

smaller and smaller, but the box remains large and unwieldy. In other words, there is very little connection between the box (the exterior) and the components (the interior). This is a flawed design.

Think of yourself in those terms. Is the exterior a genuine reflection of the interior? And, if not, why not? Your outer shell—the visible you—is it all it could be? It should be an honest manifestation of what's inside, a direct extension of the real you.

Look in the mirror.

If you have broad shoulders, show them off.

If you're tall, hold your head high.

If you're short, don't worry about it.

Don't hide the elements in your personal design that could turn out to be your greatest assets. If you have ears that stick out, show them off. If you have a large nose, be proud of it. Those are the features that make you an individual. Those are the elements that make you YOU.

That said, I am not against using the tools at hand to augment an existing design, though I would urge you do so cautiously. As we have said, men and women alike tend to obsess over their perceived

erate
your assets.

shortcomings, and as a result they go overboard when they try to address them. For instance, the most common mistake women make is wearing too much makeup, as if they were trying to hide behind a mask. When it comes to makeup, less is more.

Some men go overboard at the gym, compensating for some perceived weakness, real or imagined, and end up with exaggerated features like arms and necks that don't allow them to wear a jacket with ease.

Work on your shortcomings, certainly, but do it sensibly and with care. I remember being teased mercilessly as a child because I had big lips and was painfully thin. Now I'm proud of my big lips—they are a crucial design element in my face—and I carry my weight with pride. I've added a little muscle, admittedly, because at one point I was too thin. But my lips—would I change them? No, just as I wouldn't change my nose.

All I will say about plastic surgery is this: Your face is your face. No matter what it looks like, the pieces belong together. The moment you take a knife to your face, the design falls apart. And what's the point? Why does everyone work so hard at looking exactly like everyone else? Human beings are not created on the assembly line. We are not machine-made, not part of a mold. Instead of trying to conform to some vague ideal of beauty, we should try to be exactly who we are. Our differences make us special. Learn to celebrate them.

There are, of course, some ways to preserve your appearance and to keep looking healthy.

Take care of your skin. Exposure to sun accelerates the skin's aging process. I wish I had known this as a child. I was brought up slathering olive oil and coconut oil all over my face and body, and now, at age forty-five, I'm paying the price. These days I never leave the house without sunscreen. Kiehl's makes a great one, expensive but worth it.

Use skin cleanser instead of soap. Most commercial soaps are full of harmful chemicals, and they tend to dry out your skin. Stick to natural, fragrance-free glycerin soaps or high-quality skin cleansers. Kiehl's, Biotherm, Clarins, Neutrogena, and Aveeno make good products, but look around and find one that works for you. The right products will not only remove oil and dirt but peel away the dead skin cells. Try to use natural products.

Use a face scrub. All those dead cells on your skin can be removed with a good face scrub. I use St. Ives Apricot Scrub and it has helped keep me largely blemish free. If the dead skin cells are not removed, they accumulate and fresh skin cells have to fight to get to the surface. This makes the difference between tired, flaky skin and radiant skin.

Use a moisturizer. Unfortunately, your face doesn't have a built-in warning system, and most of us don't think about it until it becomes painfully apparent. Few of us drink enough water or get into the right habits early on. Working in an office all day dries out your skin.

Your face is

your face.

Our **differences** make us special.

Whether it's heating or air-conditioning, breathing recirculated air only exacerbates the problem. Again, look for a fragrance-free moisturizer largely free of chemicals. Prada makes an excellent facial moisturizer.

Drink plenty of water and use a humidifier—winter and summer. It can add years to the life of your skin.

If you want to get rid of dark spots, don't try it at home; talk to your dermatologist instead. A little discoloration is normal, but there are prescription bleaches for more troubling spots.

Splurge on manicures and pedicures. I go at least every two weeks. It keeps your nails beautiful, and it feels great.

Clip and trim your nose hairs, your ears, your underarms, and your eyebrows. (Yes, men should trim their eyebrows, too. And, while they're at it, clean up any unruly chest hairs).

Massage and scrub your feet once a week. Trim calluses and nails often. Use moisturizers, especially on the soles. If you can swing it, find a good reflexologist and treat yourself to a foot massage. You'll become addicted.

Learn to celebrate them.

Get a facial every three months. This is not optional. If you've never had one, you will thank me for insisting.

Take care of your teeth. You don't want to outlast them. Use a natural toothpaste (my favorite is Tom's of Maine) or gel with silica, and floss every day before you go to bed. Dental floss with fluoride is best. After you floss, rinse well with a mouthwash. And visit your dentist every six months.

Have your teeth whitened yearly.

Get your hair trimmed every three weeks. Split ends are sloppy. Keep your hair sharply designed.

I prefer showers, but hot baths are great too. Eucalyptus is wonderful, especially when you have a cold.

Find the fragrances you like, and bear in mind that each has a particular trait, so don't try to use the same for every occasion. Rosemary and mint are great in the morning, but lavender is better before you sleep. Switch your cologne occasionally, I have about ten different ones. Don't use antiperspirants because they block your pores.

When it comes to makeup...

Ladies

Always remove your makeup before you go to bed. In a pinch you can use a drop of Johnson's baby shampoo with water to remove eye makeup; it won't irritate your eyes.

When it comes to makeup, as I said earlier, less is more: nominal amounts to accent and emphasize the features. A lightly applied foundation, blush, lipstick, and a touch of eyeliner are enough. Your cosmetics should be high quality and fresh. They don't have an expiration date on them, but they become less effective with time.

Use heavier, experimental makeup when you go out. Try white lipstick. Stick to makeup that works for you. If there's a fair-haired model on the cover of Vogue wearing bright red lipstick, and you have olive skin and dark hair, chances are it's not going to work for you. If you're looking for inspiration, study the models that share your coloring and features. And take advantage of the crowded marketplace! The better department stores have plenty of makeup counters, and most of them will be happy to show you how to use their products. Don't be afraid of change, either. The face you're wearing today may not be your best (or only) face. Experiment to find out.

Gentlemen

Shave wisely and with care. Look for natural shaving gels: They tend to be more concentrated and more lubricated than commercial products. Use a razor blade, not an electric razor. It's a closer shave and it helps

Less is mORE

the better you feel,
the better you **LOOK.**

peel away dead skin, and you're less likely to get ingrown hairs. (If you tend to get ingrown hairs, both oatmeal and aloe can help.) Make shaving a pleasant ritual. I shave in a bath or in the shower in a fog of hot steam, or I fill the sink with very hot water and steam my face for a minute before I reach for the razor. You can also take a flannel cloth, dunk it in hot water, and (carefully) rest it against your face (or legs or underarms) before you shave. This opens the pores and makes for a closer shave. By the way, men should always shave in two directions. First, the face, moving with the grain, then the neck and under the chin, against the grain.

Aftershave lotions and gels are a must, and those that contain a little alcohol are best. That little sting isn't always pleasant, but you're doing your part to disinfect the skin. If you like colognes, use them sparingly. It's preferable to smell fresh and clean than to smell like something that came out of a bottle. Also, if you use a balm, don't use cologne. You don't need both. I like Davidoff's Echo, Miyake, Biotherm, and Kiehl's products. I also use Clinique's M lotion.

Men, if you insist on facial hair, be neat and artistic. Goatees, mustaches, and sideburns are all personal expressions, so design them wisely. Feel free to express yourself, but make sure you have what it takes. There is nothing worse than a spotty mustache, an asymmetrical beard, or patchy sideburns. My personal preference is for a clean-shaven face, but I'm not against facial hair as long as it's designed well.

Baldness is sexy; don't hide it. If you're losing your hair, shave what's left of it. And use moisturizers to keep that pate smooth and shiny.

The key to beauty is really quite simple: The better you feel, the better you look. If you take good care of yourself, you're already beautiful. It shows you respect yourself as a human being, and it will make others respect and care about you in turn.

There is an Italian expression, *brutta figura*, that, loosely translated, means "bad image." Italians don't like to put their worst face forward, so they always make an effort. Even if they're just going to the grocery store to pick up a little something for dinner, they take the time to wash their face, comb their hair, put on a clean shirt, and tie their shoelaces. They care about themselves. They take pride in the way they appear in public. This has nothing to do with vanity and everything to do with discipline. By looking beautiful, they are making the world a more beautiful place.

Another Italian word I love is *divertente*. The root of the word is to "divert" or amuse. It's about being *nice* and *decent* and *pleasant* and as *positive* as possible. It is about behaving beautifully toward others. A quality that I admire in a lot of the Japanese people I know is their ability to be excited about the world every day. They seem to have an unbridled enthusiasm for life. Every day is full of hope and surprise. **Few things are more attractive than a positive attitude.**

GIVE.

Be **generous.**

Improve the lives of the people around you; there is nothing more beautiful.

Be kind.

Leave good tips.

Hold doors.

Give presents.

Write letters and remember birthdays.

Let someone else have your seat, even your cab.

Give compliments. We all love to receive them and
    all too often fail to give them.

The smallest gesture can make someone's day,
    and their appreciation will likely make yours.

On that note, remember to smile, whether it's at yourself when you do
something silly, forget your keys, or trip up the stairs, or for no reason
at all. Promise yourself that you will do something beautiful every day.

Beauty is yours to give.

Love your nose.

Forget plastic surgery.

Celebrate your differences.

Try not to outlive your teeth.

Build confidence.

Be yourself, *unique.*

Smile.

As I said earlier, casualization allows us to drop the facades of dress code, ritual, tradition, and formality. It frees us to be who we are and express and live the way we feel. This is a very important paradigm shift because it allows individuals to judge and create for themselves. There is no longer a dictatorship controlling how people speak, act, work, play, or dress. I hope that in the future people will love design as much as they do fashion.

The way we dress has changed radically in the last century. The running shoe changed the way people walk. The men's tie business has dropped 40 percent in the last five years alone, and dry cleaners have less business due to the fact that suits are no longer mandatory in most businesses. The use of a single name like Madonna or Pink or Jay-Z is another example of a new global casualness. Surnames are increasingly less important. First class is disappearing in favor of business class; in fact, the most profitable planes in the United States have only one class. Jeans are an accepted, even expected, dress code in most offices now. Previously unthinkable and necessarily hidden in the workplace, tattoos, piercings, and other personalized marks are becoming acceptable by mainstream culture. The casualization that is spreading across the globe is a sign of true open-mindedness and a very positive expression of individualism.

Fashion is directionless now. Different styles are emerging simultaneously. This means that we have a plethora of choices. There are innumerable micro movements happening at once.

FASHION

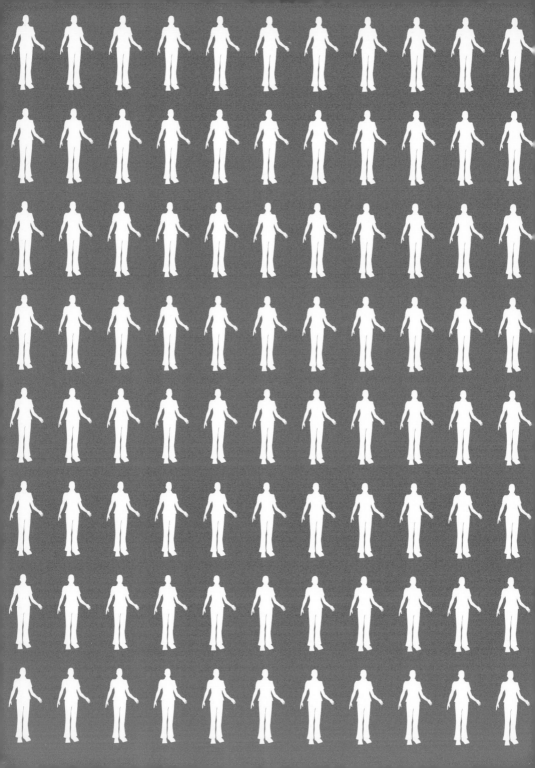

Sameness
is a **waste.**

I have designed beautiful, expressive, technologically advanced clothing, shoes, bags, and jewelry that are about flattering and accentuating the beauty of the human form in a contemporary way.

My collections work well with many different styles since they are not about historic references. While I'm the first to appreciate good design, expert tailoring, and the innovative use of materials, I'm a little wary of what we call "fashionable." The fashion industry appeals to our deepest insecurities. Assuming we don't know what we want, they tell us what to want. When we accept this, the result is mass conformity. We chase the hot new thing, and before long we all look alike. We dress alike, we use the same products, we get ideas about our homes from the same magazines, and we go to plastic surgeons for the same little noses. What happened to our individuality? The clothes we wear should allow us to express—not lose—ourselves. I was at party recently and a man walked up to me and said, "I love your glasses. I've always wanted to buy a pair like those, but I didn't think I could pull them off and my girlfriend agrees." As you know, I favor rather large (some would say outrageous) glasses, but this gentleman's well-balanced face told me that he could pull them off. So I took my glasses off and set them on his nose. He looked great. We went over to talk to his girlfriend, who couldn't believe how well they suited him.

Never be afraid to try something new. We don't always know why we like something, but no one should keep us from experimenting. Not our lovers, not our friends, not ourselves, even less the so-called arbiters of fashion. What happened to *our* opinions? **Society forces us to accept certain things without question, and this starts early— when we're young and impressionable.** Even when kids think they're rebelling, they do it en masse, wearing the same uniform—whether

to be different.

the look is goth, hippie, or gangster. Long hair and bell-bottoms or black leather and piercings—they too are conforming to a norm.

Why can't we just be our very individual selves? In the 1980s and even 1990s in New York, I remember being entertained by the looks of different neighborhoods, particularly the most flamboyant ones in the West Village and Chelsea. You'd see leather, wigs, boas, whips, chains, neon and silver, a plethora of color—sexuality worn with pride. It was an incredible outburst of creativity and individuality. Now, thanks to the pervasive influence and accessibility of L.L. Bean, Banana Republic, and Gap, people have become more conservative than ever.

Dump the brands.

Don't get me wrong—these clothing chains have done a great job of making good simple design accessible to everyone. I just wish people weren't so afraid to express their individuality. We are all so unique that it's a shame for that to be lost. I love to see people dressed in refreshing and unusual ways, people that make me stop and take notice, even if it's just of a detail: a great accessory, a daring haircut, an original combination of colors or textures.

Sameness is a waste. **People aren't interchangeable and they shouldn't dress or behave as if they stepped off a production line.** We are losing sight of who we are because a lot of us don't seem to even know what we like anymore. It's as if we've been preprogrammed to have our decisions made for us. Maybe there are simply too many options out there and we're getting lazy. I don't know but I hope that in dressing a little differently I may inspire you or others to be a little adventurous and to explore your own new look. Part of the problem stems from the fact that we are all reading the same books, watching the same movies, looking at the same magazines, seeing the same ads, and listening to the same music. That's bound to have an effect on us, so we have to be conscious of it and fight it. Don't let someone else tell you how to live your life. Dare to be different.

Now that I've given the fashion industry such a bad rap, I should admit that I have always loved fashion that is innovative, powerful, and new. I even considered becoming a fashion designer at one point and have designed clothes, shoes, bags, and other accessories. I like to push the boundaries of what we wear, just as I do with what we surround ourselves. When I design clothes and accessories, I try to incorporate new materials and technology. And it is as I approach that challenge that you must address your individual look. You can use fashion to your advantage, as a way to celebrate and express yourself. In this age of *casualism* we are free to be more expressive than at any other time in history. Let's take advantage of it!

To start with, dump the brands. Be part of the new movement: *Brandump*. Of course, you will have preferences, even allegiances to certain designers, but you should not let them dictate the way you look, dress, or feel. Think about celebrities, who can have anything they want from any designer—particularly at Oscar time. How many of them look comfortable, how many look like themselves, and how many are mannequins advertising the clothes?

Designer or otherwise, don't be afraid to mix things up a bit. **Fashion is about self-expression and evolution.** You choose whether to sink or swim; be a wallflower or be noticed. Clothes should be an extension of you, but first you need to know who you are. Usually, that's all it takes. You are already unique.

Get acquainted with what's out there and choose wisely. If you'd be more comfortable in a pair of sweatpants and sneakers, start there. Dressing well does not have to be about formality. To the contrary, I think people look their best when they are at ease in their clothes, whether it's pure physical comfort or the psychological comfort of wearing something they like or that suits them. Think of the opposite scenario: a woman, for example, formally dressed, tugging at her skirt, conscious of showing some (but not too much) cleavage—always on guard—teetering on high heels. Is that attractive? Does that look smart?

I get a lot of compliments when I travel because I use color and wear interesting, highly personal accessories, shapes, and materials. **I believe in being very comfortable**—especially when spending hours on a plane—but I also try to look good. Though I like to dress casually, I find that wearing a jacket makes me look a lot better and it has the added advantage of pockets for my boarding pass, passport, and mp3 player so I can put everything else away in the overhead and enjoy every inch of the little space I have. Although I'm technically wearing sneakers, they are beautiful, new, and clean. Like that, I am comfortable, practical, efficient—myself.

Always wear what suits and flatters you. What you feel comfortable in will always look better, and you will see that people respond to you differently. While high heels may make your legs look

To be **individual** and **creative** is far more important than being hip.

longer, if you have trouble walking or end up being flustered when you can't find a cab, you are doing yourself a disfavor. If you can walk ten blocks in stilettos or get out of a cab stalled in traffic to sprint to your next appointment, then that's you. If not, don't bother.

Men, too, can make mistakes. Try not to be too formal or, worse, too casual. Leave the Bermudas and flip-flops for the weekend. Try to be somewhat coherent in the way you dress and do introduce a little color in your wardrobe. Of course, blue and black are easier, but will anyone notice you? The guy that I sit next to on the plane that admires my pink and silver look may well wear khakis and a white T-shirt. In fact, he may have no intention of emulating my look, but he admires it on me and might be encouraged to take a risk in his own attire once he sees that it doesn't necessarily entail a sacrifice of comfort or efficiency.

The choices today are limitless and we should be rigorous about our selections. When you reach for a new item of clothing, you should feel an immediate connection to it. And when you try it on, it should be the most comfortable dress, pair of pants, or jacket you've ever worn. Clothes need to be about function and performance. They are there to serve you, to express you and make you look and feel great.

White projects light.

Black absorbs light.

Drop black.

You are unique already, so figure out who you are and dress accordingly. To be individual, independent, and creative is far more important than being hip. And "hip" is just a marketing tool, anyway. Nowadays, you can walk into a store at the local mall and buy a distressed-looking shirt and jeans with patches on them. Doesn't that tell you something about the value of hipness? Thirty years ago, we wore the shirts until they became distressed, and we patched our own jeans. Now we've lost the energy to do even that much for ourselves. Faux individualism is being mass marketed, and we shouldn't buy into it.

Recently, my sister was looking for an apartment, and I went with her. The first two realtors we spoke to looked like realtors: conservative suits, ties, nicely pressed shirts, shiny shoes. Nothing wrong with that, but not memorable—in fact, it was hard to tell one from the other. But the next one we spoke to was wearing a cape like Liberace and had the flamboyance to pull it off, so that's the guy we went with. Why? Because **I like people who have the courage to be themselves.** There is something very reassuring about that (he also turned out to be a great realtor).

If you're buying a car, there's a good chance you're going to be dealing with men and women who are dressed to sell you a car—suits, ties, skirts, sensible shoes, etc. They are wearing the uniform of their trade. If I went to buy a car, I'd buy it from the woman with the feather boa. I would like the fact that she had the courage to be herself. It is an honest expression.

I remember going to Gillette twenty years ago to try to sell them some of my ideas. I was in a conference room with a dozen people, and all of them were wearing near-identical suits and ties. I couldn't tell the engineers from the marketing people from the accountants. It told me that I was dealing with a company where people weren't allowed to be themselves. I might have been wrong, but the way these people dressed—the way they were expected to dress—sent the wrong message. I took it as a warning.

Clothes are part of the message you project onto others. They can signal something about who you are. Think about that when you're designing your new wardrobe: Who are you and what do you want to tell the world?

Color is critical. I love white and silver, bright pink, and techno colors; they represent the vibrancy and energy of our digital world.

We have the gift of freedom.

I'm finished with black. It is a tired and negative color. It does not disseminate optimism. It is no longer the radical or individual statement it once was. I have black glasses and a black watch. That's it. In 1999, I got rid of every black item in my wardrobe and opted for white for the new millennium. White is spiritual, reserved, sophisticated, and pure.

White projects light. Black absorbs light.

Black is a color of the late twentieth century. It is nocturnal, macabre, Armageddon-like. I realize I'm being very dramatic. Black is convenient, slimming, and in some contexts, powerful. I just think of the bigger picture. On a gray or rainy day, I always appreciate seeing colorful raincoats and umbrellas. Imagine if everyone had only black ones how much worse the day would feel, how heavy, depressing. Black was the spirit and signifier of punk and anarchism in the 1970s. Japan was producing black as a humble, reserved brushstroke. Black represented "no future," but we now have a bright future ahead. We can drop black.

For the twenty-first century I let go of beautiful suits by Comme des Garçons, Yohji Yamamoto, and others and started with a new pair of white jeans and one white shirt. At the time, it was hard to find white clothes for men, but since then it has become fashionable and I've been able to fill my wardrobe with everything white—shirts, pants, jackets, suits, sweaters, and shoes, along with a few touches of pink and silver. The only black I wear is my eyeglasses and my watch.

I have the same glasses in white, pink, silver, clear, and the black pair that was originally produced for the movie *Until the End of the World*.

I wear white shoes, pink shoes, and silver shoes. I have thirty pairs total (including my new line with interchangeable parts), and I choose them according to my mood. The other color I wear is gold. Gold is the new silver!

When I choose what to wear, I don't think about brands, dress codes, traditions, or other people's expectations. I dress as I like. We are lucky to live in a society that's so free and accepting, and we should make the most of it. In my wardrobe, anything goes as long as it's good quality. **Quality has a special glow, a life of its own.** In Europe, people still have their clothes tailored, and it is those details that make them look so much more elegant and polished.

When I lived in Milan, I had a friend who took packed lunches to work with him for an entire year so that he could save up for a Thierry Mugler jacket. I soon noticed that many working-class Europeans dressed very smartly, and when I looked into it I discovered that many of them were just like my friend. Instead of buying lots of inexpensive items that didn't last, they invested in quality. In this case, too, less is more.

It is our responsibility to

EXERCISE IT!

In the United States, we have the advantage of being free from history and relatively unbound by tradition. We are less likely to live with our extended families and don't have a grandfather insisting that women wear skirts and men wear a coat and tie every day. Proper, formal dressing is conformist and we should be more casual and inventive. We have the gift of freedom, and it is our responsibility to exercise it.

I stay away from modernism, minimalism, or the so-called "classic." I try to operate in the moment, to work in the first order without preconceptions, biases, or forced styles defined by the past. Design is *now*. I do not think about designing classic things because if I did, I would be using a borrowed language. "Classics" can only be designated with hindsight, and I try to do work that is relevant and beautiful now.

I like to think that more than ever people are becoming true individuals. There is a new independent spirit in the world thanks to the digital age and the technological revolution. It has made everyone aware of the entire world and provided access to a plethora of diversity of creed, race, culture, knowledge, and choice. We all have a greater opportunity to choose when we have so many options. Historically, the world was made up of collectives, pockets that remained largely unchanged due to distance and lack of knowledge. What kept us separate was the strength of tradition, religion, and ritual that also maintained and enforced conformity. Now that these institutions are breaking down, traditions are being left behind, history is becoming less relevant, and we have greater knowledge to be individuals.

Knowledge is power—knowledge is individual power!

Here's my advice:

For Women

You always look good if you stay fit.

Try to match shoes, stockings, watches, and eyeglasses.

The bigger the watch, the better.

Dress in this decade. Your wardrobe should reflect the time in which we live.

Don't wear jeans 24/7.

Dresses can be beautiful and very flattering.

High heels can be sexy, but don't torture yourself. Choose a height and style you can live (and walk) with.

Don't be afraid to experiment.

Dressing casually doesn't mean dressing as if you just got out of bed.

Don't wear business suits; they barely work for men.

Wear white all year long. A woman in white is an angel.

Skip frills. Avoid anything that's too ornate.

Wear clothes that work with your body; don't use them to hide it.

Wear contemporary jewelry.

Choose shapes that are simple, pure, sensual, and organic.

Essential for women are rings and a necklace.

Wear a watch and a bracelet so that your arms are balanced.

Dump brands.

Know your body type and dress to flatter it.

Wear all the colors you like.

For Men

You always look good if you stay in shape.

Your accessories—shoes, watches, glasses, jewelry, and so on—should always match.

Wear closer-fitting clothes, and get into shape so you can pull it off.

All your socks, T-shirts, and underwear should be identical.

Own a pair of sneakers that are special and hard to find.

Oversize is over.

Don't be afraid of color.

Buy quality, not quantity.

Break all dressing rules.

Except mine.

Do not wear pleated pants or narrow-cut pants.

New fabrics such as microfibers and all-weather garments are best when you travel—they do not wrinkle and they dry very quickly.

If you are short, wear flat-front pants, with a slight flare.

Stay away from garments that are too ornate.

Don't wear anything too retro or antiquated.

Always ask for advice or shop with someone that can look at you objectively.

Jewelry is beautiful and should be worn always. Let's emblazon our bodies.

Wear one or two rings at least.

Don't buy labels. Buy what looks good on you.

Your top should always be a lighter color than your pants, or they should match exactly.

Your shirt should always be lighter than your suit.

Be original.

Independence is the key to

GREAT

Sex should be a daily occurrence. Sex is the greatest pleasure.
We are born and brought up to be independent, we are even taught
to fight for our independence, and yet the vows of marriage are
supposed to erase all that. Just because you decide to spend the rest
of your life with someone doesn't mean you are suddenly responsible
for them, that you possess them in any way, nor that you can tell them
what to do. I love to do things with my wife, but if she wants to stay
home and paint, I see no reason why I can't go out—nor does she.
Independence is the key to a truly loving relationship and, yes, great sex.

The perfect pairing is where two people maintain their independence and the connection between them is love. We should depend on one another for compassion, companionship, encouragement, support, and consolation, but independence has to prevail. All arguments start from that loss of autonomy, from one treating the other like a part of themselves and the expectations (often unreasonable) that one has of the other. I watch this around me all the time. In most of the couples I know, one always has to control the other.

Relationships like this are depressing. The convention is that you should find a "soul mate" and that, even if you don't, you should find someone to be with for the rest of your life, and then this cocooning takes places where two people cease to be individuals and they begin to face the world as a single entity. Instead of opening yourself to experience, you cut your experience in half.

SEX

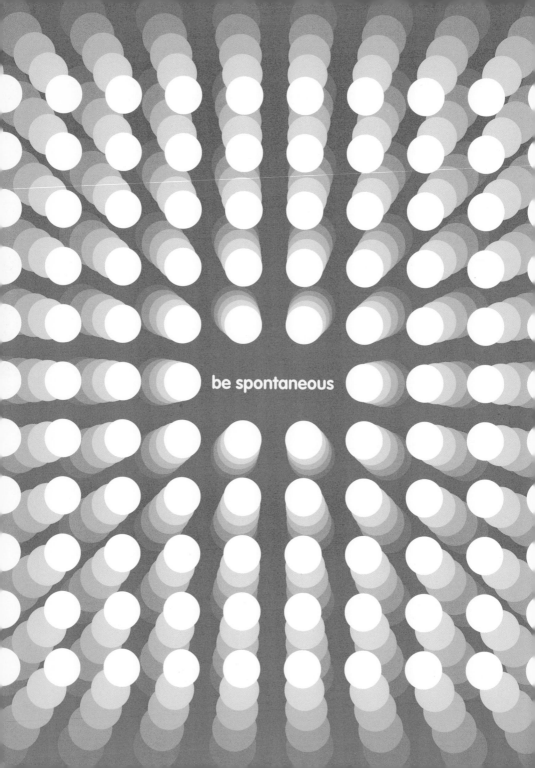

be spontaneous

People tend to isolate themselves in such relationships, the cocoon sets in, they socialize less (because one can't go out without the other, they also cut their chances of accepting an invitation in half), and they become frustrated. That frustration eventually results in a frustration with each other. When people stress that you have to "work" at a relationship, I can't help but think that you shouldn't have to—if it were natural to live in a cocoon and lose your independence it would come more easily. We must question what "work" means: to make some small compromises, to listen to each other, to embrace each other's company, to engage each other, to share, to grow, to converse, to be open, to do things for each other of our own free will, to please each other always. It is all healthy and rewarding, but it must all come naturally without even necessarily making a conscious effort. If we must spend countless months or years trying to resolve differences, we are wasting each other's time. We shouldn't have to work at it; a good relationship happens seamlessly.

If it feels like **WORK,** it's not worth it.

Possessiveness is perverse. To love someone is to let them be themselves, to allow them to live their life, to pursue their interests, and to nurture their individuality, not to confine or to be possessive of them. The key is to give them complete trust. The day you realize that you don't own anyone or anything—that you're here only for a short span of time (we are temporal beings)—is the day you can be in a successful and fulfilling relationship with your partner and with life.

In sex, something similar should happen but rarely does. Typically, one person tends to take control and sex occurs when and where that person decides. When the other fails to take the initiative, not only are they sacrificing their own impulses, they are not participating equally in the relationship. When one person takes the position of control, a dominance/subservience occurs whereby a couple's "sex life" becomes contrived and predictable. When only one calls the shots, there are no surprises. Both should call the shots and they can be and should be unpredictable, instantaneous, and immediate.

Great sex takes two. The best sex is when you're not thinking about yourself but about the other person. It's all in the mind and it's about pleasing the other. It's so simple. If everyone focused fully on giving the other pleasure, there would be no problems. For this reason, too, it is imperative not to let one person always be in control of where (not the bed again!), what (be open-minded and try something new), or when (why should it always be at night and only after the dishes are done?). The "who" is, of course, negotiable and, on that note, **don't be afraid to talk.** Say what you think, mean, like, want, or fantasize about. Fantasizing is the healthiest thing you can do for your sex life. Fantasies are normal and necessary.
I would encourage everyone to have
all kinds of fantasies and
to think about

them during sex. Don't worry what your partner or partners are thinking of you or vice versa. **Guilt is a buzz kill.** You think about all kinds of fantasies when you are with someone. Recite your fantasy in real time; it can be incredibly stimulating and erotic.

I design furniture, so "where" is something I think about all the time. Sex is a completely different experience on a couch or on a rocking chair, on an ottoman or a hardwood chair. When I design furniture I always think that it is not just for sitting. It seems that we're only adventurous when we're young and that we only try original locations when we don't have a choice. Why? When is the last time you did it in the bathtub, the woods, the sea, or the back of a car? (Although cars have become much smaller than they were in the 1970s!) And don't feel you need to leave the house, just be spontaneous, do it when and where the feeling strikes. By now, you may be catching on to yet another reason to remove all the sharp edges in your home and make all surfaces soft, sensuous, and inviting. I have had many friends who crave public sex, and yet they rarely do it because their partner is afraid. Everyone should try it. Sex should be discovered and experienced anywhere (as long as you do not get arrested).

My favorite "public" sex was in a public library (we did not get caught because

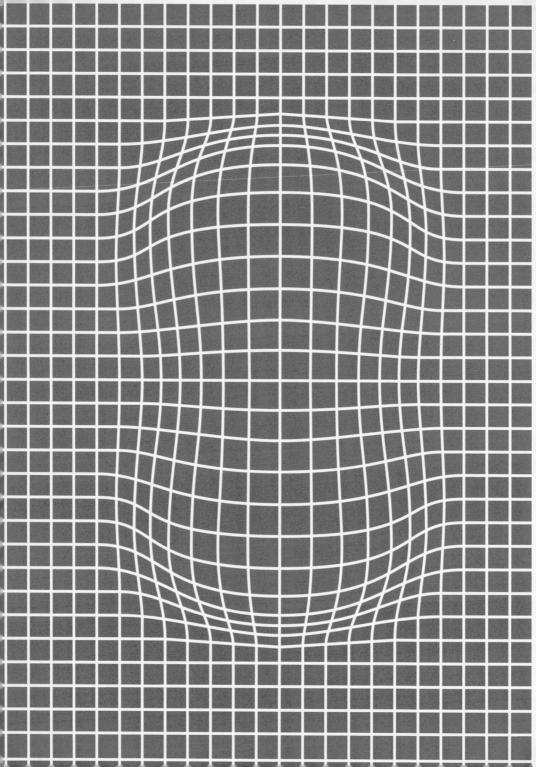

EMBRACE technology!

we were in the least frequented aisle—architecture and design).
Design your location!

Always be open-minded. You know where to draw the line, and
anything in between is worth a shot. As the saying goes, "Don't knock
it 'til you've tried it." Let go of your inhibitions. In sex, as in life, you
have to try everything at least once. Be safe but be adventurous. Be
careful but wild.

Of course, it's easier said than done. We all have our own
baggage, and our upbringing has a very strong bearing on our
preconceptions. The way to do it is to simplify. Think about yourself
and what gives you pleasure. If you have a hang-up about something,
try to address it, ideally by yourself and then with someone you trust.
I once bought a girlfriend a vibrator and a book about "how to have an
orgasm," left them at her house—with some flowers and chocolate—
and left. I had to be open-minded not to get upset about the
circumstances, and she had to try it on her own first. It worked. You
must know your body and learn it well before others can please you.
It always takes two.

Sex toys are great and, even if they're not for you, you should try
them once. Never say "no" to what you don't know. I'm designing them
now, and so are a lot of other people. They come in fun shapes and
interesting materials, sizes, and colors—and are no longer relegated
to seedy little shops. You can find them in a lot of different places, and,
if you insist on anonymity, you can find all sorts of varieties online.

WE ARE **ALL**
V⊙YEURS.

Sex toys are becoming so popular now that they are moving into more and more sophisticated and respected shops, even department stores like Selfridge's in London where there is a beautifully designed sex shop that sells everything from the hardcore gadgets to personal miniature vibrators, the famous "Rabbit" and the "Pocket Rocket." It is a first that sex toys now have name or brand recognition. Finally, things are changing so that someday we may all, without taboos, display our sex toys on our coffee tables!

I'll say it again, embrace technology: You've allowed it into your office, your kitchen, your car—even your pockets—so why not your bedroom? If something is there to improve your life and enhance your experience, why wouldn't you take advantage of it? Why even wait for someone to tell you to? While I don't want to sound like I am promoting the sex industry per se, it is interesting to note that it's where most new technologies are experimented with and developed: From photography to the home video to the Internet, the sex industry is always on the cutting edge.

I'm also an advocate of X-rated films. Watching others have sex is an amazing turn-on for almost everyone. Though most don't admit it, deep down we're all voyeurs. We can learn so much from them. They teach us positions, techniques, proclivities. If you are really liberated, you realize that sex is primordial and one of the greatest pleasures in life.

Sex is the greatest pleasure we have! And it's also great exercise. In fact, the fitter you are, the better sex is. When you exercise regularly you're in better shape, which is not only a turn-on for others but also for yourself. The better you look, the better you feel, the more confident you are. You burn about 300 calories in a vigorous 45-minute session. Feel each other's muscles, smell each other's sweat, move, gyrate, push, lift, get it on.

Sex is completely necessary. Our synapses are constantly firing away, and while we can't act on them all the time (or no one would ever get anything done) we should allow ourselves to listen to and give in to our impulses. Sex is the epitome of intimacy.

Sex should be completely spontaneous. I've known people to schedule time for sex, and as frightening as that sounds it may be better than those who lead such busy lives that they forget to have it at all. People who say they have sex one or two times a month shock me. Sex should be a daily occurrence.

Sex

177

WATCH,
learn and **PLAY.**

Finally, I'm tempted to say that monogamy is not natural, but I don't want to be hypocritical. I'm in a monogamous relationship and I hope to continue to be happy in one, but, once again, we should open our minds to alternative arrangements. But I think that we all are attracted to others and that is a natural human emotion and instinct. Remember that multiple partners or polygamy is also very natural, as is bisexuality. Again, always be open-minded and allow your sexuality to flourish, to experience, and to be free. I call it *Karfree*. When you love someone the last thing you should do is limit him or her. If my wife wanted to have sex with someone else, she shouldn't suppress that urge because she would feel guilty or because she would be afraid to hurt me. She should not be afraid to tell me, and we should at the very least be open to the possibilities. I didn't marry her to not let her live her life to the fullest.

One time, a long time ago, I was staying with some friends—a married couple—and the husband told me over breakfast that his wife wanted to sleep with me. I was attracted to her and I did. It wasn't great, but I remember thinking that maybe that's the way it should be. I thought it was remarkable that they talked about it, that she was able to express her desires and that he could be so understanding—even encouraging—of her.

Learn to trust. Trust yourself and your partner. Trust that you can share your most intimate thoughts and desires and that others will understand. Open yourself to new experiences and lead the way for others.

Have **sex every day.**

Don't stop at once a day.

OPEN YOUR MIND always.

Don't judge or assume.

Fantasies are healthy and essential.

Speak openly about sex with your partner(s).

There are **no rules.**

Be spontaneous.

Get out of bed.

public.

Don't be afraid to play.

Bisexuality is natural.

Try everything at least once.

Display your toys.

Learn to **trust.**

Don't suppress your desires.

Go wild but be safe.

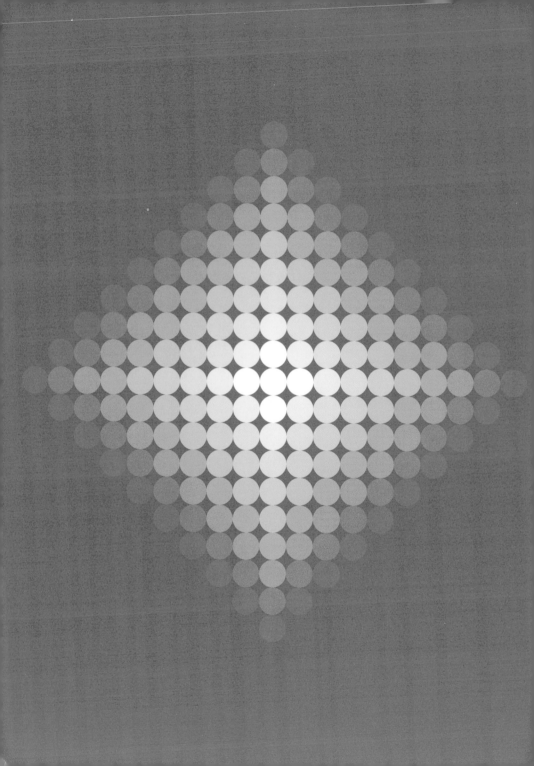

DEATH

Ours is a death-denying society, but death is inevitable and we must face it pragmatically. Too often decisions regarding death are made in haste—by distraught family members, and in times of extreme vulnerability. Whether you want to consider interment, cremation, a funeral, a wake, or a celebration of life, there are countless options that should be taken into account and made clear to friends and family in advance.

Here are the steps.
1. **Accept:** Do not fear your own death or that of others.
2. **Prepare:** Be informed and let others know what you want.
3. **Choose:** Know your options.

Don't be afraid to stray from tradition. Because people don't think about their options until it's too late, funerary professions have not been forced to evolve. If people started to think about alternatives in advance, maybe these companies would be compelled to create more interesting—and contemporary—options. Take the coffin, for instance: usually wooden, always the same basic shape, buried horizontally. Why not a clear oblong polycarbon shell-shaped designed to pierce through the soil and plant itself in the ground vertically? Polycarbonates (tough transparent thermoplastics of high-impact strength) are extremely durable and could preserve a body for 1,000 years before any decomposition would occur.

STRAY FROM TRADITION.

Why should it all be so antiquated and predictable? Why can't someone order a casket from Gucci or Prada? Why can't we have urns in new materials and original shapes to preserve our ashes in? I've designed a few contemporary urns and hopefully more and more will appear on the market until there are millions to choose from and everyone can personalize their own. And who says you need an urn? Ashes under high pressure can be made into diamonds or crafted into jewelry a loved one can wear. They can also be blasted out into space or scattered into a coral reef at the bottom of the sea.

Many companies specialize in getting ashes special places. They transport ashes out into the ocean and perform final services on boats (some even provide state-of-the-art technology to mark the exact location in the open water for future visitations). Other services will scatter ashes from the air over national monuments or holy shrines, take them into forestlands or scattering gardens to renew the circle of

Why can't someone order a

life, or even launch the ashes into space to orbit around the earth, fly to the moon, or travel infinitely across the universe. There is a broad spectrum of options from ecologically friendly cremation practices to the preservation of bodies and strands of DNA for posterity. Whatever aspect of your own death you are contemplating, consider your reasons as well as your options.

Are you motivated by cultural and religious beliefs? Is our interest in preservation after death a quest for immortality? Are we driven by an instinct of self-preservation? These are questions that are addressed differently by every culture and religion. The process of embalming as we know it today in the United States is a practice that began during the Civil War (when bodies were shipped home for burial) and has its roots in an ancient Egyptian religious rite. In Ancient Egypt the bodies of the dead were mummified and cast in gold for travel to the afterlife.

And when we think of what lies beyond, what are we hoping to find on the other side? Do you believe in rebirth or some kind of reincarnation? Buddhists, for example, think of life in cyclical—not linear—terms. Or is it a question of faith in science? Today, some believe that medical advances will allow us to fight all disease and live into eternity. Cryonics is the nascent study of the cryopreservation (preservation by freezing at very low temperature) of the human body.

casket from Gucci or Prada?

Despite the primitive state of preservation technology today, advocates feel that even a slim chance of revival is better than no chance. They speculate that in the future conventional health services will improve and likely expand to the conquering of old age itself, so that if an individual could preserve his or her body (or at least the contents of the mind) he or she might be resuscitated and live indefinitely. An admittedly compelling idea is to be preserved to witness the future.

Organ donation. Since our technology is not there yet, another issue to consider is the preservation and donation of individual organs. Organ donation can help up to fifty other people; it can greatly improve the lives of burn victims and the visually impaired, and it can save other lives. That said, your choice about organ donation is a very personal decision and one that should not be taken lightly or by anyone other than you. To that end, here are some things you may want to know about organ, eye, and tissue donation.

1. Organs, eyes, and tissues are donated only after doctors have tried everything they can do to save the patient's life, but the patient has died anyway.
2. The doctors and nurses who worked to save your loved one's life are not the doctors and nurses who will recover the organs and tissues.
3. Donation will not change how the body looks. You can still have an open casket funeral.
4. Donating organs will not cost you anything.
5. Most major religions approve of organ and tissue donation. Most think it is a gift, an act of charity.

Last will and testament. In addition to filling out organ donation cards you should consider writing a will. You should be aware that if a person dies without a valid will, statutes determine how their property is divided among relatives. Wills are made to vary the statutory scheme and may provide for outright grants or for the establishment of trusts. Bear in mind that no particular form of words is necessary in a will as long as the intent is expressed clearly.

How will you be
remembered?

Another document to know about is a living will (an advance health care directive), which is a legal instrument that is usually witnessed or notarized to state either that a person is appointing another individual to direct their health care decisions, should they be unable to do so (a "power of attorney for health care"), or to give specific directives as to the course of treatment that is to be taken by caregivers or, in some cases, forbidding treatment and/or food and water should the person be unable to give informed consent. In the Netherlands, patients and potential patients can specify the circumstances under which they would want euthanasia for themselves. The Netherlands and Belgium are, however, the only countries in the world where laws specifically permit euthanasia and assisted suicide. In the United States, only the state of Oregon permits assisted suicide.

Obituary. One detail that often escapes even the most thorough planner is the obituary. Why not write one in advance: newspapers do it, why can't you? The basic obituary contains the public facts about a person's life: their birth, their family tree, and the circumstances of their death. It can also be very personal and you can ask friends and family to contribute to it.

Here is the basic outline to follow:

I. Biographical Information: accomplishments, education, honors, hobbies, etc.
II. Survivor Information: spouse, children, grandchildren, in-laws, other close relatives, and close friends.
III. Scheduled ceremonies and gatherings of remembrance: give the time and location of any viewings, memorial services, scatterings or inurnments, or any other gathering.
IV. Contributions or flowers: Some families request that contributions be made to a meaningful organization instead of sending flowers.
V. Arrangements: This will help ease the burden of phone calls to the family. Give the day, the time, directions, or any other information regarding scheduled ceremonies and gatherings, or contribution information to florists or friends.

Grief management. Having addressed some of the issues relating to our own deaths, I would also like to share some thoughts on dealing with the passing of a loved one. While everyone's experience is different, it sometimes helps to listen to what others have to say and to know what to expect: how to predict our own reactions as well as to respect the feelings of others. For example, psychologists generally agree on five distinct stages:

1. Denial and isolation
2. Anger
3. Bargaining
4. Depression
5. Acceptance

Knowing about these stages may help you come to terms with what you are feeling as well as make you better equipped to console others in their time of grief or mourning. There are countless books—spiritual to practical—on the subject and they are worth reading. *Thanatology* refers to the study of the phenomenon of death and of psychological mechanisms for coping, and those who work in this field address not only the needs of the dying, but the effects of death on their families.

Finally, you may find solace in art—look at poetry and famous eulogies. Remember that while death is inevitable, the circumstances are not. You have the right to choose and you should exercise it. If you dread the thought of your family's grief over your loss, let them know you want them to celebrate, to play your favorite sonata, and to be together. If you have always dreamt of a burial at sea, say so. If you want a memorial in a particular place, see if you can make arrangements in advance. Don't be afraid of death, take control, personalize it, design it, make it your own, and ease the burden on your loved ones by making your desires clear.

Work

- Education
- Inspiration
- Workplace
- Finances

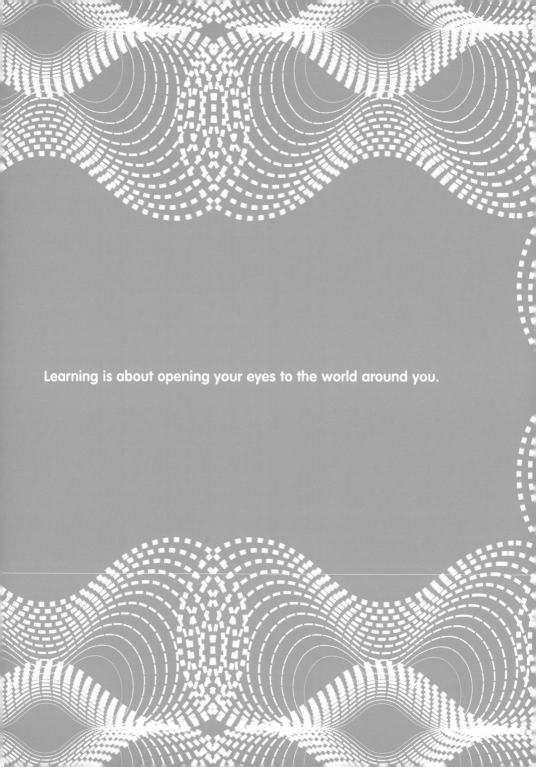

Learning is about opening your eyes to the world around you.

read.

carry books and magazines wherever you go.

EDUCATION

When I was in college, I had so many interests that I really didn't know what to do with myself. Initially, I thought I might want to be a fashion designer, but this seemed less rewarding than architecture, so I applied to architecture school. I was only sixteen at the time, having managed to accelerate my way through high school, and was summarily rejected. I ended up getting a degree in industrial design, thinking that I'd go on to get a second degree in architecture, but I became interested in engineering and suddenly found myself going off in a completely different direction. My problem was that I was interested in too much. (I no longer see that as a problem.) I was curious about art and architecture, marketing and engineering, psychology and sociology. I was hungry to learn, and I've remained hungry. I think too many people lose or give up that drive too soon in life.

Education isn't really about degrees. Some of the dullest people I've ever met went to some of the best schools. Learning is about opening your eyes to the world around you. As Oliver Wendell Holmes Jr. put it, "Man's mind, once stretched by a new idea, never regains its original dimensions." Each one of us is the architect of our own education, and education is a lifelong process. Books, movies, museums, hobbies, the local planetarium—these are there for our benefit, and we, too, seldom take advantage of them.

Education is really about doing things. Draw, paint, sculpt, sing, take pictures, learn a computer program, teach yourself a new language, do volunteer work—all of these things expand you and, in expanding you, create new opportunities.

I had a friend who lost his job and one quiet Sunday afternoon

Education

193

Find out what people are **thinking,**

found himself wandering through his local aquarium. The following year, as a result of this experience, he was on his way to becoming a marine biologist.

Education is about opening your eyes to possibility. Possibility is everywhere you look.

The next time you're at the mall, ask yourself if you really need anything, and if perhaps you wouldn't be better off going to the museum.

Read. Carry books and magazines wherever you go. You'll be waiting at a restaurant for a friend, and an article in a magazine could change your life.

Read the local newspaper. Read the editorial page. Find out what people are thinking, and why.

Even more critical, learn to listen. Even a fool can be wise by mistake, and if you're not paying attention, there's a lot you can miss.

Redesign your learning habits. **Learn to learn.**

People who stop learning stop dreaming. And if you stop dreaming, it will be hard to find inspiration.

When we are young, we are curious to know more. We know so little that everything is part of our education. But as we get older, we become more set in our ways, and more narrow-minded.

That diminishes us. We are curious about less and we have less appetite for the world around us.

Try drawing. Look at the way different people interpret the same tree.

People think learning is about amassing facts. Memorizing doesn't make you smart. I know some people who have encyclopedic memories but aren't at all creative. There are many varieties of human intelligence.

I taught for ten years and my principal job was simple: to imbue in the students a passion for what they were doing and to let each of them be who they wanted to be or who they saw themselves becoming.

In New York and in other major cities across the country, it's almost as if we're determined to stamp out individuality. I am speaking of the lemminglike desire people have to send their kids to private schools. Nowadays, it seems we're all about sameness.

We stick with our own. This polarizes not only our local communities but the world at large.

I went to a public school and it was tough. I wanted to finish as quickly as possible and in fact I graduated two years early. But when I look back on it, I realize how those years helped me become the person I am today. There were people of every race, creed, color, and socioeconomic class. It was very democratic.

and why.

SMELL

Use your senses:

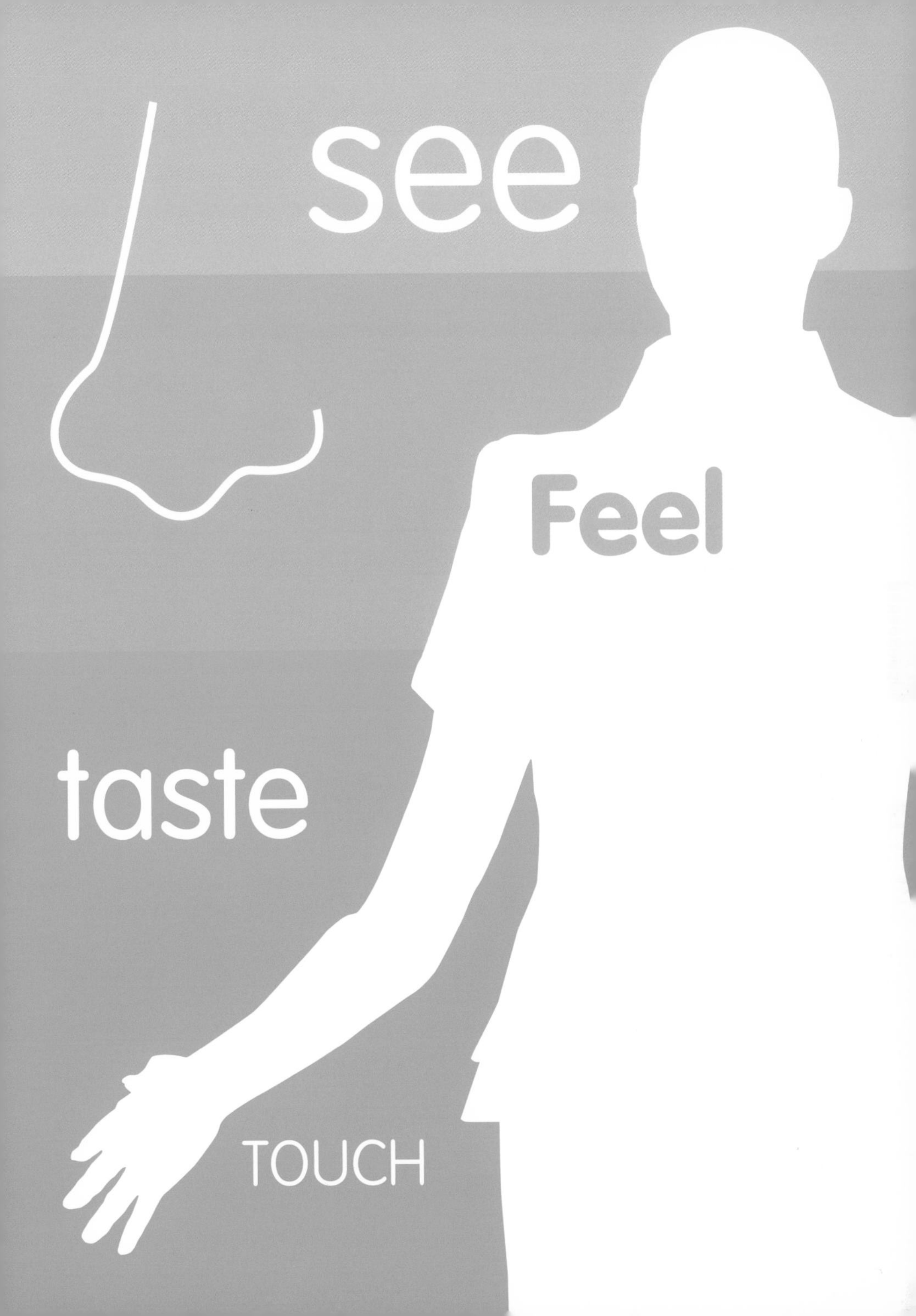
see
Feel
taste
TOUCH

Diversity is critically important. Exposure at a young age to people who are *not like you* is a very good thing. Imagine what it was like for me. My name was Rashid. My father was a nonpracticing Muslim. I don't speak a word of Arabic. The fact that I was different helped me appreciate differences in others.

People don't seem to understand that we are enriched by knowledge and, in particular, by knowing other people. There's nothing to teach and inspire you as much as people. Nothing replaces human contact and human interaction.

Join groups. Visit museums. I had a great advantage: My father introduced me to a range of great artists, from Gauguin to Warhol, at a very young age.

Use your senses: touch, feel, smell, taste, see.

Most of the great inventions come out of passion. Success comes from passion. What is an invention? It is the result of someone addressing a need in the world.

People excel only at things that awaken their passion. Try to find something you love. Conversely, learn to love what you do.

ENTHUSIASM begets

Every night, when you get into bed, ask yourself what you learned that day. Try to learn something new every day. That's education. At the moment, you may not be exposing yourself to much that is new, but if you make an effort, you will be amazed by the results.

Enthusiasm begets enthusiasm. New worlds will open up all around you.

Go to the American Museum of Natural History.

Read ten pages of a challenging book.

Watch a documentary instead of a meaningless "new release."

You could go to the mall and spend an hour looking at shirts, but think what you could learn if you spent that hour at the Museum of Modern Art.

Don't let life pass you by. Have fun, but make sure you also take the time to learn something new at every opportunity.

Being educated is being open to the fact that *you* can make things happen.

Education is learning the things that aren't handed to you.
Spend twenty minutes a day reading instead of watching TV—it will expand your world. Reading is active. TV is passive.
Reading a magazine will not only teach you something, it might increase your vocabulary. Pick up interesting new magazines.
To be exposed to the world is to grow exponentially.

ENTHUSIASM.

There are things happening in and around your home every day. Gallery openings, shows, live concerts, film retrospectives, a play by an unknown writer. Drive a few miles if you have to.

Decide to do something special every Sunday. Plan it and go

think collectively

through with it. If you don't plan, you won't do it. You get caught up with chores of the day, doing your laundry, running errands, and so on.

You have to design your education. You have to design the growth of your mind. There are three types of beings—those who create culture, those who consume culture, and those who don't give a damn about culture. Move between the first two.

From the moment I wake up, I tell myself that I am going to accomplish something that day. At play, at work, with friends, I will try something new. I want a new experience.

People get so bogged down that they stop moving forward. A problem is a challenge to participate, an invitation to act. Design is problem solving. Designers don't look at challenges as problems but as opportunities. The more constraints there are, the greater the opportunity to be creative and deliver something really new and worthwhile.

I'm not a fan of people who interpret everything as a struggle. By defining it as such they are already getting into the mindset of defeat. People define and create their own limitations.

Let me give you an example. A few years ago, a well-known designer came up to me and said, "You are so lucky! You get to design so many things. People only come to me when they want that high-tech look." And I said, "I didn't get lucky. I got interested. I looked around and saw possibilities everywhere, and I sat down and got to work." He was stunned. I guess he thought people came to me and dropped projects in my lap. But even when you're established, you have to compete. This designer had pigeonholed himself. He didn't realize that it was up to him to break out and show the world what he was capable of doing.

The next time I saw him, he had designed a chair. He found a company that wanted to back it, and he was in a whole new world of design. He made it happen.

Instead of waiting for opportunity to knock, open the door. Think externally, not internally. Think of yourself as part of the world, part of a whole, part of the universe. Thinking internally is isolating.

Think collectively, not selfishly.

Everything in your life should provide a positive, uplifting human experience.

See beauty in everything.

Some of my favorite designs popped into my head almost full blown. But others seemed to take forever. I would think, "I can't make this work," but I was wrong. In design, sometimes you find yourself forcing something to be something it doesn't want to be and then you let it breathe and it becomes what it should be.

Find a place to escape to, inside your head. I have a small quiet room inside my mind where I go when I need to get away. Nothing can touch me there. I go there to rest. I actually close my eyes and walk myself into that room inside my head, and when I get there I sit down in a comfortable chair—of my own design, of course—and take a mini-vacation. I clear out all the negative stuff. I get rid of bad moods and emerge refreshed.

It's good to go to a quiet place and think about your life. Review it. Think about what happened in the day. Forgive others and yourself.

As Blaise Pascal said, "All men's miseries derive from not being able to sit in a quiet room alone." If we don't process, we end up with clutter inside our heads, and we learn nothing.

OPEN
the door to opportunity.

That notion of addition by subtraction applies to more than just objects. Learn to clean out your head, too. Deal with the problems you need to deal with. Then move on.

At the end of the day, sit down for a moment and review everything that happened. This could be almost a form of prayer. Sit in a comfortable chair, close your eyes, and relive your day. Savor the good experiences. Consider the bad ones and why they were bad. Think about the things you might have done differently but don't punish yourself over them. Remember, this is about learning and moving forward.

I have a friend in Los Angeles, a writer, and he actually does something like this with his eight-year-old son when he puts him to bed. They review the day. They talk about how much fun he had standing in front of the class in army fatigues, telling his fellow students all about Dwight Eisenhower. Or about rehearsals for the school play and how he felt about his character "Schicky." When they're done with that, they might talk about the coming weekend—maybe going off to that trout place to see what they can catch for dinner. In reviewing the day, both the good and the bad, this eight-year-old was making sense of his life, and he'd fall asleep with a smile. Adults need that, too—maybe even more so. It's about making order. Looking for patterns. Cleaning out the detritus. Making room for new thoughts and new ideas and new feelings. And it really works. Not every day is a great day, but every day has its lessons and rewards.

This "cleaning out" process is very important in my own work. To design is to be a cultural editor. I have to empty my mind first, and only then can I absorb information, retain, and dissect it. With real-time communication, media proliferation, and our demanding work schedules, the reduction of stress and information overload has become increasingly important. Stress is a key factor in health problems, weight gain, poor work habits, and multiple emotional ramifications.

Free time, freedom, choice, creativity, intellect, and a high physiological condition and spiritual individualism are the most important goals to strive for.

Enrich your life with goals and anticipation. Look forward to everything. Look at every experience as a new one—even if it is a repeated event.

Where's the future in doting on the past? Our errors, failures, mistakes, even our moments of humiliation, were all part of our evolution, part of the learning process.

Enrich your life
with goals and anticipation.

Learn to respond to the present. If you're in the shower, focus on that. Don't think about what you're going to do when you get out of the shower.

Over the last years of traveling, I've observed how much we humans live in the past. The past is around us constantly, considering that the minute something is manifested it is the past. Our surroundings, our homes, our environments, our architecture, our products are all past constructs. We should live with what is part of our time, part of our collective consciousness, those things that were produced during our lives. Of course, we do not have the choice or control to have everything around us relevant or conceived during our time, but what we do have control of should be a reflection of the time in which we exist and communicate the present. The present is all we have, and the more we are surrounded by it, the more we are aware of our own presence and participation.

Be conscious of the present moment.
Observe everything and everyone.
Always look at things from another angle.
Support culture.
Read, write, and listen.

Inspiration is cumulative. I am inspired by my childhood, my education, all the teachers I have ever had, by every project I have worked on, by every city I have traveled to, by every book I have read, by every art show I have seen, by every song I have heard, by every smell, every taste, sight, sound, and feeling.

INSPIRATION

The words *live* and *love* are differentiated by a single letter, while *work* and *play* don't share a single letter. This suggests that they are polar opposites, and our society is certainly geared toward that idea. To play is to be frivolous; to work is to be serious. Playfulness is associated with childhood, while work is associated with adulthood, responsibility, even hardship. Work has a lot of negative connotations. Someone who works long or unusual hours is called a "workaholic," as if it's a disease. But the notion of working should not be derogatory because we should enjoy what we do for a living. If you love what you do every day, you will likely be better at it and find you are a nicer person to be around and, most important, be a lot happier. Remember that, like it or not, work accounts for at least 50 percent of your waking life!

It is our contemporary society that teaches us to polarize work:

Work vs. vacation

Weekday vs. weekend

Time on vs. time off

Work vs. life, love, and play

Yet no one spends more time on the latter, so what does that say about our society? All work, little play. Now, as I have said before, you have to work with what you've got. We can't suddenly make two-day weeks and five-day weekends, so we have to look at those five-plus days and those forty-plus hours a week and think how we can improve them and, consequently, our quality of life. Think about the present moment and make it the very best that it can be. We have to

Work should be what you **WANT** to do.

make the transition between work and play more seamless; we have to let one flow into the other and vice versa. The more we love what we do, the less it will feel like a chore; the less we constrain our time to play, the more joyful our existence will become.

Work should be what you want to do, not what you have to do. When I was a child I wanted to be a mathematician, then a painter, then a combination like Yaacov Agam or Victor Vasarely. Then I wanted to be a fashion designer. Then I finally applied to architecture school but ended up getting an engineering degree. It was brutal, but the combination of engineering, architecture, sociology, psychology, marketing, and industrial design kept my outlook broad. I did not do the typical design program at an art school but ended up with a rigorous degree. This is probably why I believe in having an expansive education, a broad view on life, and a pluralist attitude to the built environment.

Change is good. Most people, when they go through a change in life, find it intensely stressful. This is because we all have fears that keep us from moving away from the familiar. But the unfamiliar is good; it broadens your horizons, makes you a more open person, challenges, and inspires.

When I was teaching at the Rhode Island School of Design and butting heads with the bureaucracy, I felt it was completely my fault and that I was a complete failure. But when it was all over, I realized that leaving that place was probably the best thing that ever happened to me.

If you do not like your job, quit! If you are unhappy with your job, remember, there are others. You have the option to leave and find something you like better or that is more suited to you. You may not be able to do it tomorrow, but you know you will regret not trying. Even if it takes time, think of it as a journey and *map it out*. Do you need to take a training course, learn a language, or talk to a specialized headhunter? Find out what it takes and get on with it. Take the necessary steps. Never limit yourself. Investigate your options. Look at the job listings in the paper or, better yet, at your dream company! If you work for a larger corporation, talk to your human resources department about your aspirations and see if there's a better fit in a different capacity, even it is at the same company. Alternately, find out the credentials you need for your ideal job, talk to someone in the field, or sign up for night or weekend classes—whatever it takes. Remember, you are in control. If you don't like your job, move or improve it.

Where is your résumé? Is it up to date? Can it be improved? Have a friend or colleague look at it and give you some advice.

never
limit yourself.

Work on your **strengths.**

Most importantly, do not be discouraged. The reason most people stay in jobs they're unhappy with is that they are scared to change, to be rejected, to try something new. But those are also the ones who will look back on their lives and ask themselves why they never tried. Work is your life, so you have to make it all that it can be.

Don't work on your weaknesses, work on your strengths.

Since I can remember, even as a child, I have always wanted to excel at everything I do. I have always been an overachiever. I always felt that I must prevail in every situation and be the best I could. How did that become a bad thing? Being an overachiever has negative connotations, but what's wrong with wanting to be more and better? And who defines the "over"? As I said, *workaholic* is another bad word, but what's wrong with wanting to work hard? It's only bad if you lose track of other parts of your life, but if you're passionate about what you do there's no harm in giving it your all.

It seems that when you're really focused on your work, people tend to criticize you. They think you're one-dimensional. And maybe to some

degree you are, but in order to succeed at anything, you really have to throw yourself into it, and perhaps other aspects of your life will be less developed for some time, but that's not necessarily bad. You try to be well rounded, but passion drives you to your goal and you can't be passionate about everything.

Sometimes I think we criticize people who stand out or excel in a field because they make the rest of us feel smaller or less talented. Instead of feeling diminished by such people, we should ask ourselves, "What can I learn from this person?" All people who excel in their fields inspire me, they make me stronger, they show me that the world is full of possibilities. They are motivators, *catalysts*.

It's okay to put pressure on yourself: to excel, to accomplish, to succeed, to produce.

When you were a kid, maybe your parents pushed you, but now you're on your own and you have to push yourself and be intent on making it.

I think humans have a built-in need to create. Having a creative outlet makes for a happy life. Having a passion drives you to do your best.

What are my goals?

Write down your goals.

It's a good exercise. I used to get my students to think about their goals and write them down.

What is your ideal job?

What do you dream about doing?

Once my students had their ultimate goal on paper, I would ask them:

What are your goals for the next three months?

What about for the next year?

What is your five-year plan?

This made them focus. A lot of students were very pessimistic because they had no direction. But if you have a goal and you believe in yourself, it changes everything. Whether you want to be a successful design consultant or the head of General Motors, figure out what it is you want. What would make you happy? How do you want to spend more than half of your waking hours?

And even when things don't look or feel their best, don't let that crush you. Even if you hate your job, do it well. Be professional. Even if it's just a stepping stone, be the best waitress you can be. Don't arrive at work looking like you just rolled out of bed or as if you're anticipating some kind of torture. Even if you're feeling a little bored by the routine, try to keep things interesting, take on something new. Talk to others about their jobs, see if there's anything you would be happier doing or anything that you can still learn. Care about your physical appearance, too. Think of yourself as the ambassador of your company, their face to the outside world. Smile.

The most important thing is to believe in yourself. No one has ever succeeded or left their mark on the world without believing in themselves.

Try this exercise. Write down goals for every facet of your life:
I want to buy a house.
I want to fall in love.
I want to have children.
I want to be a television star.
I want to retire at the age of forty…

Then ask yourself how your goals mesh with the real world:
How am I contributing to these goals?
What am I doing to achieve them?

The best ideas are the ones that make a difference in the world. It is those big ideas that translate into success for the person behind them.

I remember having to achieve the highest grades in my class in junior high, having to graduate cum laude from college, having to become the best designer in the world. What I never realized is that there is a great deal of room for many to be the best, for many to achieve great things, for many designers to produce the best work.

In order to be good at what you do, you do not have to be so self-centered. Let go of the ego, let go of having to be the best. Accept that you must be self-motivated and not driven by the motives of success, money, and fame, but by an inner drive to create, accomplish, and produce. This is when we have real unselfish satisfaction, when we cease to define what we do by the accolades or rewards and just concentrate on the beauty and intelligence of the work, the fact that it will always be appreciated.

We are not here to please everyone else; we are here to do great things for ourselves. There is no number one. Competition can induce and inspire us to do great things but, at the same time, it can be harmful to our self-esteem and self-confidence. In the design world, as in many other professions, there is an unhealthy competition to "get" a project or client, to win the competition or the award. Once you let go of these seemingly important driving forces and focus on accomplishing things for yourself, your work will start to claim accolades and attention. Personal development is the key to a productive mental and physical state.

Think about a bicycle. It's almost impossible to balance a bicycle when you're standing still, but when you're moving, there's nothing to it. It's the same thing in life. If you have a goal, if you're moving toward something, you have a sense of direction and your equilibrium is maintained. It's all about forward propulsion. You can either sit still or go forward. You can't go backward physically, and you shouldn't go backward mentally. Why not move forward? Don't sit back and wait for the opportunity to come and find you. Remember, the career counselor can't call you. You have to make the first move.

Make it **happen.**

LOOK

for
opportunities.

When I was fourteen, I got a job in a camera store at the local mall. There was a man named Ray working there who had been a high school gym teacher for fourteen years. He took early retirement and leased a tiny store, eight feet by twelve feet. It had one little counter and only a few cameras, but anyone who came in the store realized right away that this man was passionate about photography, and slowly but surely he built an impressive clientele. I remember him saying to me one day, "I have loved photography all my life, and after fourteen years I knew I just had to do this. I was ready." Some years later, he had nine camera stores in Toronto. His passion had translated into success.

People who are passionate have the drive to make things happen. The world is a highly competitive place and only the most passionate have the drive to succeed. How can you be one of them? If your work is closely related to your interests, it will be immensely helpful. If you're looking to become a fashion model, work in a great clothing store. If you're an art student, work in a gallery. It doesn't guarantee that you'll become an artist, but maybe one day you'll manage or own a gallery. It may not be what you wanted, but it's still something you can be passionate about. If you're really into gardening and you work as a sales representative for a pharmaceutical company, change your focus—maybe you can do the same job for a nursery that sells seeds.

Of course, on the other end of the spectrum, there are plenty of people who have jobs that have absolutely no connection to the things they love, and some manage just fine. They compartmentalize. *This is who I am at work, but when I get home I build and race motorcycles.*

Work is life.

They have two sides, both of them functioning well and independently.

If there's no connection between what you love and what you're doing, you might try to find something you love in your work.

Whatever you do, do it well. There is no excuse for shoddy work. If you do your job really well, whether you are passionate or not, you are bound to climb the ladder. Good work produces results. People are appreciated. Think about how much better your job would be if you really applied yourself to it. You might as well be efficient and productive. That day will never come back. There are no do-overs in life.

Work is life. If you're going to spend so much time doing it, it becomes an integral part of who you are. What do people ask you when you first meet? They ask you what you do. People often complain about this question, but I don't understand why they're complaining. Our work defines us. It is who we are.

There's more to you than being a waitress or a salesclerk, but that may be what you are at this point in your life, and it's nothing to be ashamed of. You need only be embarrassed if you are doing shoddy work. No matter how simple or boring your job, challenge yourself to be the best at it. Someone can tell you they are a writer, but unless they're sitting down writing for several hours every day, they are not a writer. They aren't truly passionate about writing. Many people walk around saying, "I'm a writer," "I'm a director," "I'm a painter." If you have to announce it, you're not there yet. These are not just labels. Work harder. Make it happen.

Another benefit of work is that it can be a great escape. Work forces us to do something other than to focus on ourselves, our lives, and our problems.

I had an employee who was chronically sick but when she came to work, she felt better. By the end of the day, when she left to go home, you could see how hard it was for her. She had to go back to dealing with her illness.

Work gives us purpose in life, motivation. When we are occupied and absorbed by our work, we are less likely to suffer from depression. The more we do, the more we want to do, the better we become at it. I find it helpful to have a lot of things to do at once as I get twice as much done in half the time. And I know a lot of people complain that when they have too little to do they have a hard time getting anything done at all.

Work is work. Keep your personal issues personal. You are being paid to do your job, you should do it well, even if you feel underpaid or underappreciated. It may not be inspiring work, but you have to make it interesting. It is your job and you have to take pride in what you do. In Italy, even the kid behind the coffee bar is proud of his job. He has been there as an apprentice, learning to make the *espresso perfetto*.

Take pride
in your work.

When you return six months later, he's been promoted; he is making the coffee on his own and is visibly proud of it.

I love to see people taking pride in their work. To see that the man behind the bar is as interested in making the perfect cup of coffee as I am in creating an object is very exciting. The way he looks at you, the way he handles himself, the way he sets that cup down in front of you. It's all about the full experience: the right mood; the right atmosphere; the taste, temperature, and quality of the coffee; pleasing the customer; and taking pride in a job well done.

In the United States, we are often faced with a waiter who is just killing time before he gets a gig on a new hit television show. That's understandable; he has to make a living, but he should also try to do his job well until he gets the one he's after. Even if a big producer is not likely to see him there, it would make the whole experience more pleasant for his customers, and he would feel a lot better about himself. In addition, if he is open and friendly, someone may ask him about his other interests and possibly even introduce him to someone in the film industry. It's amazing how one thing can lead to another and, often, the chain is set off by a single nice gesture. One of the most powerful producers in Hollywood today owes his success to being noticed by a studio executive because he was such an efficient valet. That executive gave him his start, and the rest is history.

Remember those old gas station commercials? Six guys would rush out to pump your gas, wash your windshield, and check the tire pressure? What happened to those days?

When you walk into Nordstrom's, the sales staff is polite and attentive. For whatever reason, they are motivated. Perhaps it's because they work on commission (there's nothing wrong with being motivated to make money), but in so many places, you can't even get service. People can be so surly it can really ruin your day, and that's not the way the face of a company, a shop, or a restaurant should be.

In Japan, you walk into a shop to buy a two-dollar bottle of shampoo and you are treated like visiting royalty. This is as it should be. There are plenty of places to buy shampoo, and they should be happy to get your two dollars. And they are. They are focused and attentive and it makes a difference. It makes you feel appreciated, and it makes you want to come back.

There's a pharmacy near my home where I literally can't get anyone to help me find anything, and when I do, they do it grudgingly. Why would I go back there? I'd sooner walk a few more blocks where I can count on reliable, professional service.

Taking pride in your job and doing it with devotion will change its character. If you've tried this and you remain unhappy, it's time for a change. Look out for opportunities. Get a new job.

WORK should be renamed:

MY LIFE
MY PASSION
MY CONTRIBUTION
WHY I'M HERE
or...

WORKSPACE

Make your office work for you.

Your workspace is the best place to experiment with streamlining and efficiency. Even if the basic structure is defined by the company you work for, there are many things you can do to improve your own station. When I approach the design of a hotel room, I lie on the bed, close my eyes, and start from there, the center of the room, myself. I am the guest; my primary reason to be in the hotel is to sleep—that's the most important element. From there, I can start to address other issues: getting out of bed, where my feet first make contact with the ground, how it feels, how it might be improved. I reach out from the bed and see what I find. Is the light switch nearby? What's the ideal alarm clock? Would it be convenient to open or close the blinds from my bed without having to go to the window? And so on.

Unless it's your home office, chances are you will have a limited sphere in which to redesign, but no matter—a lot can be done there too. Again, **start from the center: you.** You are sitting down, and this is your office. What do you need to be the most comfortable and efficient? Is everything you want or need within reach? Is there anything there you could do without that would yield more space for you to think? Have you introduced any uplifting colors so that you're not further sedated by the monotony of the generic office?

Many people find the future and technology frightening, and film representations don't help. Most movies about the future are dark and apocalyptic, but I see the future as bright and completely liberating.

configuration.

Re

Think how far we've come in the last decade alone. With a computer or a PDA, most of us can work not only from home but from just about anywhere and at any time. This is an incredible development. The Internet and cellular phones make us reachable so that we are more and more free of the constraints of an office.

RECONFIGURATION: YOUR DESK AND COMPUTER
In the bedroom, we started with the bed; at the office, everything revolves around your chair. Could it be more comfortable? Would you be better served by a chair that had wheels? Do you not have a choice about the chair you sit on? What can you change? Even a cushion to support your back or something to put under your feet can make a

significant difference. Are you at the appropriate height for your desk, computer, and keyboard? What adjustments can you make there? Try raising your keyboard or changing the angle on your computer. See how it feels to face a different way. Move your monitor from left to right and choose the vantage point you prefer.

Before we move on to the surface of the desk, look underneath it. Or maybe you don't need to. Maybe you know you're storing junk down there. Are there empty boxes or convoluted masses of wires under there? Take them out.

Remember how you are affected by your environment. Doesn't the tangle of wires under your desk nag at you a bit? Do you notice the cables when you put your feet under your desk? Do others see the complex web you are harboring under there?

Could you use a little **streamlining?**

Most of us could. The wireless, paperless office is not quite here yet, and many of us are caught in a messy transitional phase. You may have wireless Internet but need to plug into a printer. Your desktop computer may have more cables coming out of it than you know what to do with. You may have added peripherals, all of which come with their own wire and space requirements. Stay late one day and see what you can improve. Get under that desk to tie up excess cables and see if there are any you can do without. Plug everything into a single power strip. Simplify where you can.

Keep your desk neat, clean, and empty. This means you are staying on top of everything. Remove all the clutter. Designate a place for everything and store as much information as possible on the computer—not Post-its all over the computer! Train yourself to write notes in the computer directly—even on digital Post-it notes if you feel that makes the transition easier. All new addresses you receive should go straight into your address book or database. If you learn to do this consistently, you will never wonder where you put that card, wrote that number, or stuck that darned Post-it.

Set up hanging files for anything you need to keep a hard copy of: projects, bills, contracts, and invoices. Try not to file anything you don't absolutely need. Once it's in the file, it will be harder to go in and clean it up, and the superfluous papers will get in the way of finding the important paperwork when the time comes. Try not to have a "miscellaneous" file because you won't be able to keep track of what's there. If you really have to, file things alphabetically within it.

Again, look around. What's on your desk? What needs to be on your desk? If it's not there because you need it today, find another place for it.

Keep your desk **neat, clean and...**

empty.

Try to keep your space—and your mind—clear. Where is your lamp? Is it providing all the light you need? Is it the right kind of light? Are you getting enough sunlight? If your office doesn't have windows or you live in a place where winter days are short, you may want to consider using a full-spectrum lightbulb that provides the closest approximation of real sunlight. For many people who suffer from SAD (seasonal affective disorder), it literally makes the difference between night and day.

What else is on your desk? Is the telephone close enough that you can use it in a comfortable position? Do you use it so much you should consider a headset? Can you see when you have messages? Have you allocated a place (ideally on your computer) to take down

What sort of **IMAGE** are you projecting?

messages? Do you have a good stapler, pens, clips, and other supplies neatly stored and within reach? If not, think about what you need and dedicate slots in your drawers for each. Whatever doesn't need to be on top of your desk should not be there. Computer, telephone, lamp, pen, and paper, that's it. The rest can disappear. Files belong in drawers and reference materials on shelves. The clearer your desk, the clearer your mind is.

And what about when someone comes to see you? What sort of image are you projecting? Are you the picture of efficiency? Try not to eat at your desk. Read the paper online so it doesn't take up any more room than it has to. Make your appointments back to back so that you also have longer stretches in which to focus on your other work. Prepare for your meetings in advance. Be courteous and dedicated, but don't let meetings go on any longer than they need to. Give a full hour and give it your all. You rarely need to do more.

EFFICIENCY: WRITING AND FILING E-MAIL

Read incoming e-mails thoroughly before you reply. And watch what you say when you do hit that "send" button, because it's there for posterity. Don't answer in haste or you could get into trouble. Efficient as e-mail is, sometimes nuances are lost and the message is read differently on the receiving end.

Try to answer all your e-mails the day you receive them, and keep track of those you don't get to so that they don't get buried the day after. Create an efficient filing system within your e-mail program, too. Set it to delete the trash as often as possible and get rid of outdated mail frequently. Empty your inbox once a week.

Have only one global e-mail address and one phone number (use a global cell for everything), and forget a hard-wired phone line. Now you can even talk long-distance over the Internet for free! If you have a fast Internet connection and speakers on your computer, try downloading the software at www.skype.com.

Use your proper name for your e-mail address. It's efficient and logical. Don't bother with business cards; just tell people your e-mail address. Once you have theirs, e-mail them any other contact information they may need and have them do the same. That way you both have the data digitally and can copy it to your address book or PDA without fear of losing it or getting numbers wrong.

Be careful about your spelling. In this day and age, there is no excuse for typos. Clean it up. Show you care. Turn spell-check on in your e-mail, Word documents, and anywhere else you find it. Read over everything you write at least once. Keep a dictionary nearby, ideally online.

While you're there, switch on to a word-of-the-day program. This will ensure that you introduce some new words into your vocabulary and expand your horizons every day. Imagine if everyone did it. If we all heard each other's new words, we'd all be learning more, using a greater variety of words, and expressing ourselves even better.

English is the fastest-growing language. *Webster's Dictionary* lists 450,000 words, while the *Oxford English Dictionary* boasts 615,000 (not including technical and scientific terms) and with 200,000 in common usage there is really no excuse for any of us not to learn a few new ones. I've been known to invent words to describe phenomena that existing words don't do justice to and, recently, at a trade fair, I noticed some (for example, Blobject, Technorganic, and Digicraft) were used by others in reference to trends. The next time you're writing something, open the thesaurus and see your options. Learning a new word that you didn't know existed is incredibly gratifying.

~~eling~~ spelling.

OFFICE INTERACTION

Don't let your responsibility for your workplace stop at the edge of your desk. Caring about the rest of the office is like caring about the street where you live. Be neighborly: Create a recycling bin for excess paper, incorrect photocopies, fax confirmations, and so on. When you see there's no more coffee, make some. If the copier stops working, call the repairman. If you're going out to get something, ask your colleagues if you can pick up anything for them.

In Athens, people open the shutters of their shops early in the morning, and the first thing they do is hose down the sidewalks and the street. In New York, I am responsible for the sidewalk in front of my shop and for an additional nineteen inches of street beyond the curb. Don't ask me where they came up with that nineteen inches, but I take care of it gladly. It helps me be a good neighbor.

I think we should **work harder at being better neighbors.** I hate fences. I hate dividing lines. It makes us less neighborly and less of a community. I hope we can become a borderless society, where fences are only imaginary. The wireless version of fences: chainless chain-link fences. That would make the world a better place.

Treat employees, clients, and even competitors the way you would like to be treated by them. Never say, "I could have done that." You didn't do it. Someone else did it. They worked harder. They got there first.

TIME IS PRECIOUS.

Improve your attitude. What is your own attitude toward your workday? What effect does it have on others? At my local Starbucks, there's a kid who is always in a good mood. He is full of energy and always has a kind word for his customers. I always leave with a smile on my face. That kid is paying it forward. He is making the world a better place. If you can reach out and make the people around you happy, it will pay off a thousandfold.

I'm not a huge fan of charities. I never know where the money is going, or where it will end up. But I try to be generous with the people whose lives I know I can do something to make better. If I'm in a cab and the driver is particularly pleasant (and a good driver), he will get a generous tip. Think about it. That puts him in a good mood. He takes a lunch break and is nice to the man behind the counter. The man behind the counter goes home and is nice to his wife. They make love. Nine months later, a baby is born. Good begets good.

TIME/CREATIVITY/MOTIVATION

Of course, to get ahead, you shouldn't waste time. When we're young, we feel we have all the time in the world. But one day you're forty years old and you're still unsure of where you're going. It's never too late to change, but why wait? Anytime is a good time to make your dreams come true. You will live long and prosper, but only if you are the architect of your own destiny.

Time is precious. When the sun goes down this evening, that's it for the day. That day is over. It is not coming back. Young minds are so young and fresh and capable, and yet we don't always take advantage of our youth. When we're young, we have the hunger and stamina for everything. Find your dream and chase it with everything you've got. Youth is resilience: You fall down, you get up. That's the key to success.

All work has a creative component. If you haven't found it, look for it. Sometimes it helps to talk about what you do with someone else. It's the things we do well and frequently that we most often take for granted. Make a pact with yourself that you will do the very best work you can manage.

If you think your job is hopeless or that you'll never find nourishment in your work, find a hobby that fulfills you—that will make up for it. Find something that creates balance in your life. Don't worry if you're doing it for the first time—do your very best at it. The results might surprise you.

Never be satisfied with your work.

Multitask. **Do six things at once and you'll never be bored.**

Perseverance, consistency, and rigor breed success.

Know everything about your current project, and forget it all when you approach a new one. Clean your slate, clear your cache. Leave history in the past where it belongs.

Being famous should not be a priority—work should be.

Pay your dues. Learn from others.

Work is life. Do it well.

DRIVING TO WORK

Now that we've addressed the office, think about walking out—and into your car. Short ride or long commute, make it the best that you can. It's every day, twice a day, many hours a week. Particularly if you commute, it is imperative that you assess your current situation. You may just make a few improvements but, unless your car is new, chances are you could do with an overhaul. Let's start from there. This weekend, have a seat in your car—while it's still parked in your driveway—and look around. What do you see?

Do you like what you see? What you feel? What you smell? What you hear?

Are the windows clean?

Think how nice it is when they are crystal clear and shiny.

Do you hate the upholstery?

If you're spending upward of ten hours a week in your car, you should rethink it.

Are the seats sinking? Does your back hurt?

Can you have the seats fixed or add back support? A simple cushion that's ergonomically shaped to support your lower back can make a huge difference, especially when you're sitting in traffic.

Is the leather sticky in the summer?

Cover it in any color you want. Look into having slipcovers made; that way, you can also wash them.

Could the car use a good vacuuming?

Do it yourself, find a kid in your neighborhood who wants to earn a little cash, or go to the car wash.

Does your car smell like your dog?

Unless you are the only ones who ever use the car, air it out.

If you have a dog or other pets that travel with you on occasion, keep towels and blankets on hand. Once you've cleaned the car, you can keep it that way by covering as much as possible. Sheets or blankets are easy to shake out and wash; the interior of the car is not. If you do this diligently, the car will stay relatively clean, and you won't need to worry about picking up all the hair on your coat next time you put it on the back seat. And think of your passengers. Make this a welcoming and pleasant experience for them too.

Does your car smell like your DOG?

Let's get back to the driver's seat. Do you have everything you will need when you're driving?

For You

Water, tissues, mints

A spare set of sunglasses

Change for the tolls if you don't have an electronic toll-paying system

Maps. If you travel a lot, consider a GPS (global positioning system)

Cell phone charger (and your phone)

All the music you could possibly want to hear

If you spend a lot of time in the car, a great thing to do is to download pod-casts of your favorite radio programs, ones you've missed or ones you'll never tire of listening to. Audio books are another good idea.

For the Car

Do you have a spare tire and all the gadgets you need to change it?

Do you have window-cleaning solution and paper towels in the trunk?

Do you have the necessary registration, insurance forms, and maintenance manuals in case something goes wrong?

Be prepared. Think of your car as your living room. Care for it as if it were an extension of your home. Get regular tune-ups and make sure it's always in its best operating condition. A smooth trip to work is a great way to start your day, and a clean, organized, functioning car makes a great first impression.

Read the fine print on your credit card statement.

Design is about efficiency and seamlessness. Managing your money should be too. Learn to streamline every aspect of your finances.

If you have debts, go to your bank and ask them to consolidate them into one program. They can take your loans, your mortgage, your car payments, and your credit card bills, and put them under a single umbrella. It is much easier to handle one payment, once a month.

Read the fine print on your credit card statement. Most people aren't aware that interest rates can become usurious. If you don't like your rate, switch it. Credit card companies are very competitive. Some offer incredibly low rates for the first six months. Take them up on their offer and remember to move on when the rates are subject to change. But, again, remember to read the fine print. (Some of them have grown wise to this practice and will take measures to discourage or confuse you.)

Know your LIMITS.

Pay all your bills online. Your local bank can help you set this up, and can even show you how to make regular, recurring payments. You'll save on stamps, paper, and time, and you'll never be late on another payment. In addition, you'll be able to keep track of all your accounts from the comfort of your home.

Know your limits: never spend more than you can afford. Live within your means, not on credit.

Don't go into unnecessary debt for a luxury item. Save the money first.

Don't be SEDUCED

by things you don't need.

The time it takes to save for that dress/pair of boots/cashmere sweater will also give you time to think about whether the item is really worth it. If you're lucky, the price may have dropped by the time you're ready to make your move.

Don't be seduced by things you don't need. Avoid impulse buying. Avoid sales. When you see something you want to buy, and it brings a genuine smile to your face, ask yourself if you're still going to be smiling in a month. Think before you spend.

Carry only one credit card and, if you can swing it, one that's also an ATM card.

Make sure you are not paying a service fee at your bank. The banking industry is as competitive as the credit card industry, to which it is inextricably linked. Any bank that is still charging you a monthly fee should stop being your bank today.

Check your bills. Cable rates, long-distance charges, and cell phone plans change every day, but no one is going to call you to offer you a better deal. Go to websites that offer comparisons of different plans. Make a point of calling the various companies at least two or three times a year and asking them if they can do better. You might be pleasantly surprised. If not, switch to another carrier.

Think about the ramifications of mishandling your finances—that will help keep you on the straight and narrow. Stress, collection agencies, more stress, unpaid bills, even more stress, and so on and so forth. Don't go there. Stay on top of your spending if you don't want your quality of your life to suffer. Healthy finances = less stress = better quality of life.

If you need help getting out of a financial black hole, there are people who can help you, and they're at your local bank. Some financial "experts" advertise in newspapers and on television, and no doubt many of them are reputable, but be careful: If their promises seem too good to be true, they probably are.

If you can't handle your credit card, lock it up. If you can survive without it for three months, you've earned the right to start carrying it again. Try not to reach too often.

Play

- Travel
- Color
- Shopping
- Sleep & Dream

New cultures =

New interpretations =

LIMITLESS

POSSIBILITIES

TRAVEL

I love traveling. I'm passionate about it. I love the whole tumultuous experience of it; the cab rides, the airports, the labyrinthine security measures, the flights, the cities, and, of course, the people— humanity in its myriad shapes, sizes, and endlessly variegated colors. To travel is to be inspired, to open your eyes and learn to see the world the way others see it. New cultures = new interpretations = limitless possibilities.

When I go to a place, I must immediately work there, produce something as my message or comment or contribution to that place. I get overwhelmingly inspired, and I cannot stop thinking of what I could do! I love the whole world. I love diversity. I love how others are driven to create, to contribute, and to project energy into this world. And I love how technology has given us access to the world, because it gives us the opportunity to be inspired by every culture, by everyone, everywhere, and anytime. This is the omnipresent new age in which we live. **More choice, more exposure, more information, more exchange,** perpetual communication, so that we become a vast, inspiring, single world! Hopefully, one day we will have a peaceful world, one religion (the religion of respect and love for each other), and a positive creative intellectual future: a nutopia!

I love globalization. It is not frightening but rather inspiring and interesting. We will eventually have one world, one beautiful place without prejudice, borders, or wars. All ideas, styles, and forms will merge and then fragment into diversities based not on cultural traditions and myopia, but on the new autonomy of individual diversities and our creative minds.

Vacations shouldn't be about lying on a beach, daydreaming.
Not all day, anyway. Even if you're passionate about scuba diving, why not take the time to do something different at the end of the day? Visit some ruins. Drive to a nearby fishing village. Look at an ancient church.

The problem with vacations is the way we define them. The word *vacation* has become synonymous with doing nothing. I usually travel for work, but I always take an extra day for myself to immerse myself in the culture. I look at the architecture, visit markets, enjoy the local cuisine, practice the language. If I have an extra day in Prague, Seoul, or Tenerife, I take advantage of it. I know it's part of my continuing education.

A vacation should be about regenerating ourselves and learning. Before you travel anywhere, do a little research. Find out what the country is about. Become familiar with its history and its people and the things that make it unique. The more you learn in advance, the richer your experience. Pick up a few phrases before you get on the plane. Bring a phrase book. There's also a great little book called

A vacation should be about **regenerating** and learning.

Point It in case you're at a loss for words. It shows pictures of everything from different types of beds to exotic fruits and vegetables.

Bring appropriate music.

One thing I don't do on vacation is phone home. Never. Instead, I write Megan extensive e-mails about my day. I give her a synopsis of my day. What Milan is like: the weather, some memories of living there twenty years ago, descriptions of the interesting people I've met in the course of the day. It's a narrative, and the writing of it crystallizes it for me too. I talk about the food. Exactly what I ate: the pasta; the pecorino cheese, which was the freshest I'd ever had. That great bottle of Barolo and the way it opened in my glass and was transformed by the end of the meal. And Megan writes back: What she painted, where she went to pick up lunch, or who she went to the movies with. We are sharing our days with each other in a fresh and intimate way. We relive it as we describe it.

I always come back from a working vacation feeling reenergized

Bring appropriate
mu

and full of ideas. **Vacations should be nourishing.** Doing nothing is the most draining thing in the world. Why do you think people always return exhausted from vacations? Because they've done nothing, they haven't absorbed anything new. Maybe the difference is that I don't travel to get away from my life. Travel is part of my life.

I travel more than most people, and it isn't always a labor of love, but I always make the most of it. As much as we've been liberated by technology, there comes a time when a face-to-face meeting is essential. I travel constantly to meet clients and vendors, give lectures and attend fairs, oversee existing projects and secure new ones. But I also travel to meet people and be continually inspired.

As a child, in the 1960s, I remember watching *Star Trek* and being convinced that by 2005 we would be beamed from one location to another using molecular transfer. I thought that I would be transported from my living room into another living room on the other side of the globe within nanoseconds, but obviously we're not quite there yet.

We're limited by the fact that the planes we fly on today were developed in the 1970s. We still fly at subsonic speeds of less than Mach 1 (761 mph) because we are flying with antiquated equipment and technology. Considering how important speed has become in our everyday lives, we should be flying at supersonic speeds of Mach 3

Make travel easy, pleasurable, **seamless.**

by now (three times the speed of sound). Then traveling would be so much easier, more immediate. We could fly from New York to Tokyo in four hours. Instead, we continue to spend a lot of time on planes and in airports in order to travel far shorter distances.

So with all this time on planes, in airport lobbies, lounges, buses, taxis, and so on, what do we do? How does one make travel easy, pleasurable, and seamless? Here are some suggestions that will ease your experience:

Never check luggage if your trip is less than six days. Having had my luggage lost four times in one year on various airlines, I decided long ago to use only a carry-on bag. The best carry-on luggage consists of two bags—a rolling suitcase (forty to forty-five linear inches is the maximum allowed) and an oversized briefcase (a tote or carry-on without wheels) that fits perfectly onto the arm of the rolling one. This way you can navigate the airport with one hand completely free.

A good twenty-four-inch suitcase with wheels is ideal. And make sure it's sturdy. One time when I was flying from JFK in New York to Tokyo, the flight was canceled and the airport closed for security reasons, leaving around 20,000 people out on the street. We had to walk back to Manhattan and it took seven hours. I had poorly designed luggage with no wheels. Bear in mind unforeseen changes when preparing to travel.

Carry-on luggage enables you to change flights if necessary or advantageous, to make connections at the last minute, and to act quickly in case of delays or cancellations. **Smaller luggage keeps you light, organized, and highly mobile.** When you have all your possessions with you, you won't find yourself lacking. When you find

Know your

yourself spending the night where you were only meant to stop over, you won't be without your contact lens solution, a change of clothes, or that essential prescription. When you master packing a smaller bag, you never have to wait for your luggage, lose it, or find that is has been damaged. You can forget about luggage carts and porters, and you'll never bring too much on a trip. Packing lightly forces you to edit, and editing makes life a lot easier.

My suggestion is that bags should be semirigid, not hard or totally molded. Softer bags have some flexibility for packing and tend to be lighter. I use both, but I choose a molded hard case (polycarbonate is best) for my oversize luggage on the occasions that I do check a bag. Of course, if you are carrying anything fragile, a hard case may be advantageous; just keep in mind that the space you are allocated will be much more rigid, too.

One thing to consider is that luggage is very personal and an extension of you. When you travel, it's also part of the first impression you make, whether on a business associate or your long-lost cousin. I am always shocked that the majority of bags I see at check-in or the baggage claim are not only generic (black or grey) but often of really poor quality. No matter what airline you fly, you know your luggage will be beaten up, thrown about, and occasionally even rained or

luggage.

snowed on, so **buy something sturdy that will last.**

I suggest buying high-quality luggage that is a reflection of you, an extension of your clothes—your style. I find luggage on the whole is very conservative, dark, boxy, and utilitarian, but not terribly efficient or new. When I was last in Japan, I found a really interesting suitcase that is bright fluorescent orange with a black and white camouflage pattern printed on its hard molded case. This luggage is not only very much in keeping with my philosophy of self-expression, but it is

Make it
yours.

extremely recognizable, so I see it immediately as it is coming off the conveyor belt.

And that's another important point: Know your luggage. Who has time to ponder which of the myriad rectangular black boxes coming off the conveyor belt is theirs? More often than not, we are tired and groggy when we land, so why complicate matters? Wouldn't it be better if you barely needed to focus to see that fluorescent bag out of the corner of your eye? And imagine what a different place the airport would be if everyone started adopting my philosophy. How much better would you feel if after an overnight flight to Europe you were greeted on the other end by a splash of color? Think about every aspect of the experience.

If you don't have the time or resources to find original—and individual—luggage, don't worry. Make it yours. **Add a special tag, stickers, patterned masking tape, or simply tie a colored ribbon on**

the handle. Whatever color you like, one that makes you happy, one that you identify yourself with, and, most importantly, one that will individuate your bag!

Another bag I bought recently in London has a clear polycarbonate window where you can slip in a photograph and really personalize it. Imagine a picture of your dog, your own face, your favorite painting, a symbol, or even something a little subversive. I thought that was a good idea because you can always change it, according to your mood or the purpose of your trip. You could even use it to hold a map so that it would always be within reach.

My wife Megan has a transparent orange rolling suitcase. It's fun because you can see her clothes inside—just like looking at the x-ray machine—and I love the comments we get when she uses it. **Beauty + Humor.** I'm sure I've said this before but it bears repeating: Think of the effect you have on others—whether it's smiling or holding a door, wearing a combination of eye-catching colors, or carrying an accessory that makes people stop and take notice.

When I travel I use only one credit card. This card is my ATM card and it has my frequent flyer number on it. I rarely use cash when I am traveling. I buy a cup of coffee, even a magazine with my card. I've also used it for taxis. I go to a local ATM if I really need cash. At any ATM in the world you get the best exchange rate. Forget foreign exchange places and traveler's checks (they are so last century), and forget bringing cash with you. This way you can have only the slimmest wallet. I carry no more than four cards in my wallet: my green card (ID), my driver's license, my credit/ATM card, and my health insurance card. **Simple.**

WHAT
TO
PACK

I try to bring no more than two pairs of shoes—one dress and one running shoe. I work out while I travel (I run the treadmill six miles a day), so I always bring a good running shoe. My dress shoe is actually a casual running shoe that I designed because it is so comfortable and we walk so much when we travel. But it is no ordinary shoe; it is a strong reflection and extension of my tastes and aesthetics. It is a wild pair of kicks! **Make that one pair of shoes expressive of you.**

Megan always brings a "hybrid shoe"—something that is super-comfortable yet dressy, both interesting and sexy, for example, a pair of Miu Miu shoes in metallic aqua green and medium high heels that are rubber (almost running shoes).

Sometimes I'll bring my silver Hugo Boss boots that are my techno faves. I also bring a bathing suit that crosses over into workout shorts and/or sleeping gear.

In my wardrobe, I have thirty pairs of white cotton socks, thirty pairs of white underwear, and thirty white 100 percent cotton T-shirts of the same brand. I also have ten microfiber T-shirts exclusively for traveling. This way I can quickly pack four of each for five days away (the clothes I wear are for the fifth day). **I can pack in minutes.**

I only wear white, silver, or pink, so my wardrobe and packing are simple. But regardless of your color choices, my recommendation is to buy microfibers or clothes that don't wrinkle easily. Microfibers (extremely fine filaments) are amazing because they keep their shape, breathe well, are lightweight, repel rain, work year-round, dry quickly, and are extremely comfortable. I bring with me microfiber T-shirts with EC2 Qwik-Dri for wearing under my clothes and to exercise in as well as to wear on the plane. You can wash them in the sink, and they dry very quickly so they never smell. I bring one suit (microfiber or cotton), one coat (microfiber raincoat—my favorite, by Moschino, is super lightweight, can roll up in my luggage without wrinkles, and is too cool for words). I bring one lightweight sweater (100 percent cotton, never too warm), two pairs of pants—white jeans and white dress pants—and two shirts. I may bring lightweight gloves and a white cap if I am off to a really cold climate. **The only extraneous item I may carry is a gift.** I love to give gifts to friends and clients.

My toiletry bag has the best balm and shaving cream I can buy, always in tubes, no glass, no aerosol cans, and no bulk. I carry a plastic travel spray for cologne that I designed, floss, and lip balm. For women, three-in-one makeup is best: blush, lip, and eye. I bring a toothbrush dedicated to traveling, a micro comb, and a small tube of natural tooth gel. That's it—no nail  clippers, no manicure sets, no creams, ointments, vitamins, nothing. Leave all that at home—you can get anything you really need locally, wherever you are. If you eat well, vitamins and supplements are completely unnecessary. Remember medication if you need it.

If you want to be comfortable while traveling on a plane, make sure that you don't wear a belt (put it into your luggage) or anything else that might set off the metal detectors. Pockets should always be empty; carry jewelry in your carry-on, and wear a watch that is soft and casual that can pass through the passenger screenings.

I try to consolidate technology. I use a laptop, a mobile phone, and an mp3 player. That is it. I make sure I have one small lightweight book, a sketchpad, and several pens.

Don't buy magazines and bring extra bulk with you.

Don't buy at duty-free shops. Remember that cosmetics are no longer duty free. Ask yourself if is worth saving a few dollars for extra bulk and extra weight.

Use your phone or watch to wake you up. I recently missed an incredibly important meeting in Naples while staying at the Vesuvio five-star hotel because I never received a wake-up call. No matter how many stars, service is always questionable in hotels, so the less you rely on it, the better off you are.

buy duty-free.

When you are on overnight flights, do not let the airlines dictate your sleeping or eating habits. Sleep when you normally would and eat when you normally would. I have always found it ridiculous that I am woken up two hours before landing, for a breakfast that I don't want, at what is actually one o'clock in the morning New York time. Why can't I just have a small cocoon of privacy where I can be alone and control my own needs?

When you arrive anywhere, it is most important to get onto the local time zone immediately. If I arrive in Europe at eight in the morning, I have a coffee and go to work. I don't think about the time in New York.

YOU CAN

afford to travel.

I then have lunch and dinner at the right local time and I stay up that first night until my typical bedtime of about midnight. Yes, it is a long and tiring day, but I wake up perfectly without jet lag. I am adjusted to that place and feel energetic and positive the next day.

If I fly to Korea or Japan, I typically continue on New York time until I arrive and change the time when I land. When I go to Japan I arrive in the early evening, so I have dinner and go to bed at midnight—and wake up at sunrise in Tokyo feeling 100 percent.

If I have some important appearances, I sometimes FedEx my clothes rather than carry them so they arrive in the hotel prior to my landing. Additionally, I sometimes wear one suit and do not pack any and have it dry-cleaned locally. You really can travel empty-handed.

If I can stay looking good in all white, you can definitely look sharp while traveling in all black.

I would live in the hotel if I could! A hotel must emphasize the pleasurable, the sensorial, and the experiential with heightening experiences that are forever memorable yet seamless. In this digital information age, a hotel should embrace the global village and create a cosmic sense of well-being. It should represent our new millennium. Design and architecture can play an important role in intensifying this reality by providing and maintaining our enjoyment of living—a direct experience with the energy and modus of the time. I see the future of our world crossing all the aesthetic disciplines so that design, art, architecture, fashion, food, and music fuse together to increase our existence and bring greater pleasure to our material and immaterial lives. Our motivations should focus around our conscious collective memory and a desire to fill it with ideas that move between art and life. As art takes its ideas from everyday life, I hope that everyday life will take its ideas from art.

At the hotel that I designed in Athens, guests enjoy the comforts of high design and an artistic, technological, and poetic experience. It is an intimate hotel that focuses on positive energy, culture, design, and art. Rather than replicating the experience of every other hotel in no matter what part of the world, this one shows guests a memorable time, unlike any other, anywhere else in the world. The spaces are conceptual and include art, ideas, technology, visuals, textures, and colors that are intrinsic to our being.

Don't think you can't afford to travel. Start saving up now.

Be a sponge. Ask questions. Learn.

somewhere new.

Shopping is
MORE
POPULAR
than
SEX.

SHOPPING

In America, shopping has become more popular than sex.

We live in a capitalist society, and we all reap its benefits. The agenda is clear—sell things, grow rich, sell more things, grow richer. The problem is not necessarily overproduction (or that we're overwhelmed by choice); it's that most of what is on the market is poorly designed, uninspiring, antiquated, unnecessary, obsolete, or just not relevant to the time in which we live. Everything from ugly newspaper boxes on city streets to the awkward bathrooms on airplanes, depressing office spaces, ubiquitous bad garden furniture, poorly designed public transportation, and the abysmal automobile—I could go on and on. Design is in its abecedarian stage. It is only now becoming the subject of common interest, and only recently are businesses and corporations taking it seriously. **We will always need objects, but everything in our lives should offer us an experience** (hopefully heightened), touch our emotions, give us pleasure, increase our aesthetic landscape, and make us feel alive and excited to be alive.

Like the syntax of our language, objects too change over time, and so we should learn to be liberated of things, to use them, have them for a while—during the time they afford us exceptional experiences— and then to feel free to move on to the next, the upgraded, the "new and improved." Whether we like it or not, we live in a material world, and ours is a consumer society.

Remember to add by subtracting. For every new object or thing you attain, you must (ideally) dispose of the same object or thing. For example, if I buy a pair of socks, I must throw away a pair of socks. I have abided by this rule for two years now. I will admit it's difficult, but

I have managed to maintain this equilibrium for some time. If you have a true "collection," this may be the exception. I recall receiving a beautiful vase as a gift for a lecture I gave, and I kept it on my kitchen table for two days to observe its presence in my world. Knowing I had to remove this vase or another, I contemplated it and decided not to keep it.

In the future we will lease everything. We will own nothing, or very little, and just lease beautiful things! This is the natural progression: We lease cars, we lease houses, and soon we will learn to lease everything, experience it for a short while, and go on to the next. We will create a hyperconsumptive, forever dynamic, and ever-changing human condition where everything will be cyclical, sustainable, biodegradable, and seamless. This is Utopia, this is freedom, and this is Nirvana. Objects will

Sales are about **SED**

exist only if they give us necessary, new experiences. Design will use smart materials, be more human, softer, more intelligent, less expensive, hyperfunctional, and poetic. There will be a strong awareness of and societal need to use and experience products, designs, objects, and spaces that are contemporary. We will lose our obsessive focus on the past. We will all understand that the past is not better—the future is. Starting today, we should live in the world now, not the world of yesterday.

Sales are about seducing the consumer, and often there's a reason that certain items didn't sell during the season. Look at all those great deals hanging in your closet that still have tags on them. The next time you see a SALE sign, beware. There are, of course, some bargains to be had, but if you wouldn't be prepared to spend twice the sale price, it's probably not something you need. If you are only considering it because the price is so low, think about what you are replacing, what you could get rid of to make room for this new item, and that usually answers the question of whether or not you should be investing in it. Remember also how many things you buy on sale. Does it really make more sense to spend twenty dollars five times instead of a hundred dollars once?

I've noticed that Europe isn't quite as sale-crazy as America. They have sales, but they don't seem to be as popular as they are here. I noticed that European shoppers are more circumspect about sales.

ICING the customer.

They seem to understand that sales are really about making you buy things you don't need: the coat that almost fits, the pants you might wear some day, the shoes that are only one size too big. What seems impossible to pass up will come back to haunt you when the time comes to clean your closet.

Be an educated consumer. The good news is that the proliferation of information, particularly on the Internet, has contributed to our educated consumption. We are more aware of what we buy; we can easily research just about anything we want or need on the Internet:

Get **SMART.**

We can make price comparisons, learn more about a company or its competitors, and read other consumers' ratings and reviews. In the last several years I have bought a car, a house, a toilet, several appliances, books, music, and clothes on the Web. Going to most shops is boring and time consuming, and most stores lack the infinite choice of the "global mall." I really shop only when I travel. I look for those rare goods not available near me, things that are still unique to that particular place. Otherwise, I go to cyberspace.

One time I needed a hammer and went to the local hardware store to pick one up. The parking lot was full, so I ended up driving around looking for a parking spot for twenty minutes. I had to park several blocks

SHOP online.

away in a lot that charged by the hour (that took another forty minutes). Then I had to walk ten minutes in the frigid wind to reach the hardware store. It was so crowded inside that it took another fifteen minutes before I even found the hammers. I found myself looking at twenty-five hammers, all of them very similar. Since I don't know much about hammers, I went off to enlist the help of a salesperson. I found one, but he knew even less about hammers than I did, so I ended up settling on one that was both aesthetically pleasing and solid. I returned home with my hammer, fighting traffic. It had taken me over three hours to buy a twelve-dollar hammer. I decided I would buy my next hammer online.

Get smart. Shop online.

Some of the best deals can be found on eBay.

Some of my favorite stores:

Arango
Dadeland Mall
7519 SW 88th Street
Miami, FL 33156
+1 305 661 4229
www.arango-design.com

Karim Rashid Shop
137 West 19th Street
New York, NY 10011
+1 212 337 8078
www.karimrashidshop.com

Moss
146 Greene Street
New York, NY 10012
+1 212 204 7100
www.mossonline.com

Aero
419 Broome Street
New York, NY 10013
+1 212 966 1500

SFMOMA Museum Store
151 Third Street
San Francisco, CA 94103-3159
+1 415 357 4035
http://store.yahoo.com/sfmoma/

La Difference
125 South 14th Street
Richmond, VA 23219
+1 866 452 3433
www.ladiff.com/

Unica Home
7540 South Industrial Rd
Suite 501
Las Vegas, NV 89139-5965
+1 888 89 UNICA
www.unicahome.com

Colette
13 rue Saint-Honore
75001 Paris, France
+33 1 55 35 33 90
www.colette.fr

Vise Versa Shibuya
Picaso 347 6F, 1-23-16 Shibuya
Shibuya-Ku, Tokyo, Japan
+81(0)354641110

Idee
6-1-16 Minami Aoyama
Minato-Ku, Tokyo 107-0062,
Japan
+81(0)334096581

Firma Casa
Al. Gabriel Monterio da Silva, 1.487
Sao Paulo, Brazil
+11 3068 0377
www.firmacasa.com.br

Benedixt
Pca Benedito Calixto
103 Pinheiros
Sao Paulo, Brazil
+11 3062 6551

Purves & Purves
222 Tottenham Court Road
London W1T 7PZ
+44 (0)20 7580 8223
www.purves.co.uk

Conran Shop Chelsea
Michelin House, 81 Fulham
Road
London, SW3 6RD
+44 (0)20 7589 7401
www.conran.com

Conran Shop Marylebone
Marylebone High Street
London, W1U 5HS
+44 (0)20 7723 2223
www.conran.com

Corso Como 10
Galleria Carla Sozzani
Corso Como 10
Milan, Italy
+39 02 653531
www.galleriacarlasozzani.org

Spazio Sette
Via dei Barbieri 7
Rome, Italy
+39 06 6869747

Move Up
163 Queen St. E., Suite 103
Toronto Ontario M5A 1S1
Canada
+1 416 304 1196
www.moveup.ca

Fluid Living
55 Mill Street, Building 8
Toronto, Ontario M5A 3C4,
Canada
+1 416 850 4266
www.fluidliving.com

BD Ediciones de Diseno
C/ Mallorca, 291
08037 Barcelona, Spain
+34 93 458 69 09
www.bdbarcelona.com

Vinson
Passeig de Gracia 96
Barcelona, Spain

Asplund
Sibyllegatan 31
SE–114 42 Stockholm, Sweden
www.asplund.org

Svenskt Tenn
Strandvägen 5
Stockholm, Sweden
+46 8 670 16 00
www.svensktenn.se

The Frozen Fountain
Prinsengracht 645
1016 HV Amsterdam, The
Netherlands
+31 (0) 20 6229375
www.frozenfountain.nl

COLOR

At one point in my life, I was having panic attacks. The doctor asked me what I saw when I had a panic attack—he wanted to make me think visually. I told him I felt as if I had huge chains wrapped around my torso. He suggested that I stretch out my arms and try to break the chains, and I did. Somehow, in imagining those chains—in really seeing them—they became more tangible. I saw them, grabbed them, and lifted them over my head. I freed myself. It was a question of identifying the problem and focusing on it. Now that I could see the chains, they were less threatening. I realized they weren't all that heavy, and I set myself free.

We must never underestimate the power of perception or of the visual realm. Our minds are extremely susceptible to everything we come into contact with and we can control the positive input in many ways. Color is the most obvious and immediate. Sir Isaac Newton, who invented the first color wheel by splitting white sunlight into red, orange, yellow, green, cyan, and blue beams and joining the two ends of the color spectrum, also associated each color with a musical note. Since then, many artists and thinkers have studied the psychological effects of colors—hence the generally accepted, and somewhat cliched, definition of reds, oranges, and yellows as "warm" (awakening and exciting) colors and blues, greens, and violets, as "cool" colors (which evoke peace and tranquility). I tend to favor vibrant colors, whatever the hue, because they exude positive energy.

Color is life. Color is one of the most beautiful phenomena of our existence. For me, color is a way of dealing with and touching our emotions, our psyche, and our spiritual being.

Color can really shape a mood.

Some colors are strong; some are soft. What is important is the specific hue, tint, and saturation of each color and how they work together. No one should be afraid of color—experiencing it is a spiritual phenomenological euphoria. Look at the countries that lie along or close to the equator and how they use color and how color use becomes more muted as you move toward the poles. Look at all of our cityscapes: gray. Only signage is colored, as if we need an "excuse" to use color: for kids, for signs, for fun, but never for buildings themselves.

Color can really shape a mood, a place, or an object. Color has always been a great interest of mine. I wrote my thesis on cultural color biases. We are biased by our natural surroundings. The Adriatic

Why are COLORS perceived as

and Mediterranean seas inspire different "blues": the latter is more cyan. Nordic countries favor the colors of nature that are less rich: muted brown, beige, and cream, while Egyptians prefer the dark red of the henna that flows down the Nile. I know that color has the potential to alter our state of mind. Color is emotional. I am drawn to (and predisposed to use) colors and designs that convey very positive emotions, energy, pleasure, and well-being. Colors in general can be uplifting, but I am especially interested in the colors of our contemporary world: pink, of course, and techno colors—colors that have the vibrancy and energy of our digital world, the colors of computer graphics. My designs seek to imbue a sense of being alive and hyperpresent, a knowledge that we are here on this earth, in this moment. The use of color is instrumental to this goal.

Anything that can have a color should have one! For centuries we were limited to earth tones. Vegetable dyes could be vibrant but were hard to come by. Even pure white wasn't an option until cotton could be bleached. The preponderance of black and other noncolors had a lot to do with the fact that you could make fabrics darker but not lighter. When things began to be mass produced, they were made of a single consistent color and it was rarely questioned. In 1980 I was working for a Canadian phone company (Mytel), and I struggled to get them to

FRIVOLOUS?

move away from the then-standard beige of business telephones. It was as if using neutral tones made technology less threatening. I would have liked to make the speaker button blue, but that was simply too radical. This may seem silly now, but look how long it took the computer to change color. Apple created a splash with the iMac, and still the bestselling color was the most sedate—"blueberry."

And why are colors still perceived as frivolous? Like the Mac "flavors," countless times I've heard my products referred to as "candy-colored," and my new shop as a kaleidoscope, a "candy store."

Color has the ability to

IMP

Maybe this shouldn't bother me, but I still don't understand why the transition is so hard to make. Computers and other appliances have vacillated between warm grays and cool grays for decades. For generations, refrigerators have come in one of three "colors" that are not even colors; they are the same old noncommittal, innocuous, inconclusive, noncommunicative off-whites with names like "almond" to make them sound more exotic.

Coming back to the computer, wasn't it fun to see people walking around with those first colored iBooks? Didn't the rounded edges and the color make the computer seem like a completely different creature than the old gray elephant sitting at your desk in the office? The brilliance of that design was that it really communicated the new role of

ACT
our state of mind.

the computer in our lives. It was no longer a giant processor of data or the ball and chain that anchored you to your office, but a fun, new, personal object—one that you would want to have with you at all times. A player of music, a keeper of photos, a way to keep in touch with your friends, get on the Internet, and so on. It spoke of our unique time.

Objects are becoming more personalized, and soon they will be perpetually customizable. To really be expressive we have to have choices. In the future there won't be any "standard" noncolors, and everything will be customizable. We're already doing it with cars. Of all the butterfly chairs I made, the pink one is the number one bestseller.

Revel
in color.

I hope that's a sign that we're moving toward a greater receptiveness to change the chromology of our environment.

It's easy for me to say that you should add color to your life. I'm the one with the white walls and floors and furniture of my own design. I realize it isn't always easy to work with color, especially within an existing environment and perhaps without the confidence of knowing what to mix and match. You neither want to clash nor match. You can't have too many disparate colors but you should also stay away from a scheme of predictably matching colors. Perhaps you have to start small. Practice by bringing flowers into your home—tulips, for example—and each week try a new color, even one that doesn't immediately appeal. See how it works in your space; move the flowers around the house. Do they look better in sunny areas or as bright accents in the darker ones? Is a particular color working nicely in a specific spot? Enough that you might consider a little more of that color? Do it in steps. Once you work your way to your preferences, everything will fall into place.

Colors have the power to impact our state of mind. A certain color may agitate you, or there may be a particular color combination that you find particularly soothing. There is such a thing as color therapy, and it's a very interesting concept. If we can learn to recognize what works for us, we can create nurturing, inspiring, or even therapeutic settings for ourselves.

With high-tech polymers and other innovative materials, today you can have any number of colors in any number of shades on absolutely anything you can think of. Even our building materials could be made in bright colors. Imagine the landscape we could create then!

There are literally millions of colors, so instead of having a single favorite color—or favorite song or favorite book for that matter—see how many you can embrace. The beauty of this farrago in life is the broad diversity and choice in everything we come into contact with. **I love color and use it fearlessly,** as a way to drive emotion though physical objects and spaces, to express, motivate, and inspire, but also to question, to challenge. I hope this will inspire you to experiment with it for yourself.

Maybe all it takes is a paradigm shift. Diana Vreeland observed that "pink is the navy blue of India." If we could stop fearing color, feeling that we have to justify it or that it draws too much attention, we could embrace a whole new palette and be forever changed by it. Even if only in small ways to start with, **use color wherever you can.** I hope you will introduce it to your home (if you're not ready for colored walls, start with fabrics, objects, and details), wardrobe (find a color and make it yours, don't be afraid; if you love turquoise, wear it), and accessories, (try a yellow wallet—it will make it a lot easier to find, too). Color is there for you to revel in.

SLEEP & DREAM

I can remember being five years old and wanting to remember my dreams. When I was a child I had a book and a pen beside my bed, and the second I woke up I wrote down my dreams. I even made doodles and drawings of them. My mother told me it was a good exercise for learning to remember my dreams. Eventually, after drawing and jotting down my dreams for about three years, I found myself just remembering them. I had trained myself. Now I can still remember eight to twelve dreams a night. I love being able to recite them and to think about them throughout the day.

I dream of ideas and projects and sketch them when I get to my office. One of the dreams I remember best is that I had a boxlike folded structure that, as I opened it, unfolded into a city. Each plane had buildings, facilities, and people on it. I was spreading open the literal city of my dreams—a *nutopia*.

Dreams are a powerful way

Dreams are a very powerful way of releasing issues and frustrations; they are also a way of fantasizing, creating, and challenging. To recall your dreams is to let go. Once I recall the dream I do not repeat it. I do not dream the same subject again unless the catharsis hasn't run its course. If I have the dream a few times, I realize that it is because I haven't dealt with the situation, haven't drawn it, or haven't remembered it well enough in my consciousness. Once it is clarified, I am free.

Sleep well. Here are the ideal sleeping conditions:

1. Think of the bed as a sanctuary. It is a spiritual place for repose and reenergizing. It is a sacred place to stay young and healthy, to be strong, alert, focused, and happy the next day.

2. Whatever your means, buy a decent mattress. Medium to firm is best (just as you should always use a soft toothbrush—they really should make only one type).

3. Flip and rotate your mattress once a month.

4. Ideally, **you should have 100% cotton sheets.** If you can spring for it, try 100% linen. Covers should be cotton, not wool or synthetic, so your body can breathe.

5. Make your bedroom a place for rest only. Do not put anything in the space that could potentially bring you stress or anxiety.

of **releasing frustrations.**

6. Do not have a TV in your bedroom, and do not read books or work before you sleep. Do all these activities in another room if possible.

7. Have dimmable lights in the bedroom so that you can adjust your eyes gradually. **Design your lighting to set the right mood.**

8. Pillows are critical.
Use only one good-quality pillow. Do not raise your head too high; it will strain your neck.

9. Burn incense or use a candle or incandescent (not fluorescent) light. Color-changing lights are also nice to create a meditative mood.

10. A kiss is the best send-off to a good night's sleep.

11. Never face the back of the bed toward the door or entrance to the room.

12. Try to sleep in absolute darkness.

13. Wake up with daylight. It's the natural way to rise. It will help your sleep cycles.

14. Always wake up to music, never to alarm sounds.

Ideally, wake up to very low, soft, comforting, and inspiring music. Lately, I have been waking up to *What Is Hip*—the remix project—with subtle remixes of Seals and Crofts, America, Todd Rundgren, and others. I also listen to Stanley Turrentine, Diana Krall, Natalie Cole, Diana Ross, Miles Davis, Jean Michel Jarre, Philip Glass, Donald Byrd, Roy Ayers, Moby, Aimee Mann, Paul Anka, Julie Cruise, and some trip hop groups like Thievery Corporation. You can also find a good commercial-free channel on Internet radio and hear some new music.

15. Disregard famously productive people who brag about sleeping only four hours a night. If you want to look ten years younger, sleep seven to eight hours a night. If your life affords you a siesta, then you can split these hours between day and night.

16. Wear no elastics, buttons, or zippers to bed. Silk and cotton are the best fabrics to sleep in, and sexy too.

17. Keep your bedroom beautiful, clean, and neat. A single bunch of flowers, a nice scent, high ceilings, and soft furniture with rounded edges all help to create balance and serenity for your psyche.

Dream well. Here are the ideal dreaming conditions:

Always sleep in slightly cooler temperature. I have the best dreams when the temperature drops.

Have sex. Make love with your partner every night as the perfect nightcap—then you will dream really well.

Try to keep your bedroom for sleeping only. Before you go to sleep, avoid reading disturbing news or watching violent films or shows. Read the news in the morning (on the Internet) and watch violent films at a matinee.

Do not drink fluids for two hours before you go to sleep or you may be forced awake to go to the bathroom. This will disturb your dreams. Dreams need to be completed in order to be fulfilled, and getting up disturbs sleep patterns and REM cycles.

Make your bed every morning so that when you go to bed it is perfect. Order is good for the soul and the subconscious.

GOOD

NIGHT.

CALENDAR

YEARLY

- See your doctor for a full checkup.

- Go to the dentist two times.

- Whiten your teeth.

- Check rain gutters for clogs.

- Clean all windows inside and out.

- Check the batteries in your flashlights, smoke and carbon monoxide detectors.

- # Reevaluate your year (pros and cons)
  and make goals for the year to come.

- # Buy a new wardrobe
  and donate your old clothes.

- [ ] Buy one new pair of shoes and throw out the old ones.

- [ ] Repair any leaks in your house.

- [ ] Keep a first aid kit at home (and one in your car) and update it every year.

- [ ] Hire a certified personal trainer to reevaluate your fitness routine.

- [ ] Throw HUGE dance parties (New Year's Eve, Birthdays, and Anniversaries).

- # Take a vacation:
  Visit a foreign country, a different one every year.

SEASONALLY

- Vehicle maintenance: oil change, check tires, etc.

- Turn on/off your outdoor water supply.

- Clean unwanted leaves, branches, and weeds off your lawn.

- Reevaluate, rearrange, reorganize: furniture, storage areas, etc.

- ## Spring and fall cleaning:
  Declutter: clean your closet, garage, and any storage areas; give away items that can be reused, recycle what can be recycled, and trash the rest.

- **Engage in seasonal sports:**

skiing, snowboarding, skating, swimming, diving... enjoy the change of seasons!

■ Unsubscribe to all mailing lists and magazines you do not want/read.

MONTHLY

■ Get a haircut.

■ Pay bills online.

■ Get a facial.

■ Get tickets to the theatre.

• Reconnect
with an old friend or make a new one.

☐ Go to hear live music or a poetry reading.

☐ Go to a museum or art show.

☐ Rotate and flip your mattress.

☐ Clean your car inside and out.

☐ Clear out your refrigerator.

☐ Choose one home improvement to do.

• Create something:
a painting, a sketch, a poem;
sew, knit, sculpt...

- **See an independent film**
  at a local theater.

- Read a biography or a great literary classic.

- Put your photographs into an album; throw out the ones that don't make the cut.

WEEKLY

- Do laundry and keep your clothing organized by color.

- Go grocery shopping with the whole family or, better yet, visit your local farmer's market.

- **Try something new**
  (every Sunday).

● Pamper yourself:
Get a massage, a manicure, or pedicure.

☐ Exfoliate your pores and apply a mud mask.

☐ Do something creative.

☐ Call your family.

☐ Have a dinner party.

☐ Take a yoga class.

☐ Incorporate a good stretching routine into your workout and do it once a week.

● Go dancing
(club, disco, ballroom, samba...).

- Make a to do list for the day and try to cross everything off.

- Keep a journal.

- # Eat healthy:
  Don't forget to eat breakfast.

- Tidy up your living space for ten minutes.

- Do something nice, be gracious, and smile more.

- Return phone calls and answer all e-mails.

- Listen to music.

- Cook a meal from scratch.

Exercise (four to five days a week).

- Make time for peaceful reflection and renewal: meditate, relax, do yoga.

- MAKE LOVE.

- Learn a new word in your native language.

- Learn a new word in a foreign language.

- Read the news online.

- Live in the moment, enjoy the process.

Reevaluate your day:

Analyze and neutralize unpleasant experiences, learn from them and clear your mind before going to bed.

LIFE CYCLE

MONTH 1
Lift your head, stare at faces, respond to sound.

MONTH 6
Ready for solids, sit up, and roll over.

YEAR 1
Use one or more words with meaning.

Understand simple instructions.

Become aware of the social value of speech.

Take a few steps.

YEAR 2
Start talking about yourself.

Begin to understand abstract concepts.

Learn to swim.

YEAR 3
Demonstrate heightened awareness of self and others as members of a family, as well as curiosity about how families of other children live (How can Sara have two mommies?).

YEAR 5

Get a pet. Learn to care for something, even a plant.

YEARS 6–8

Read constantly.

Draw, paint, make models, do crafts.

Play video games (they increase mental and physical response mechanisms and can increase intelligence).

Watch documentaries.

Go to openings and be exposed to crowds.

YEAR 9

Start writing a daily journal or diary.

Rearrange your room.

Choose your own clothes.

Talk to strangers (as long as you are with someone you know well).

Hikaru Nakamura, 10, is the youngest chess master in the U.S.A.

Arfa Karim Randhawa, 10, a promising software programmer from Faisalabad, Pakistan, is believed to be the youngest Microsoft Certified Professional in the world.

YEARS 11–14

Learn to play a musical instrument.

Start to play competitive sports.

Learn to speak a foreign language.

YEARS 11–14

Start to read books for pleasure.

Invent things.

Exercise and eat healthy.

Get braces.

Experts say Neanderthals were fully developed by age 15.

YEARS 14–19

Do something creative.

Start a band.

Get a part-time job.

Learn how to cook a meal.

Go to a museum.

Build your own website.

Make digital movies and music.

Travel as much as possible.

Don't stop drawing, reading, and learning.

School should be the priority.

YEAR 16

Get a driver's license.

YEAR 18

Legal age for a tattoo in most states (wait until you are 25—then you know what you can live with the rest of your life).

YEAR 20

Believe in yourself; know what you believe and why. Truth matters.

Develop good spending habits. Learn to budget and invest.

Turn the TV off.

Start an exercise routine.

Make good/true friends and keep them.

At age 20, Mies Van der Rohe designed his first independent work, the Riehl House.

YEAR 21

Legal drinking age. Learn to appreciate alcohol, not abuse it.

By age 23 Andy Gibb had a total of nine hit songs in the Top 40, resulting in four gold records and one platinum record.

Beethoven was the first composer to become freelance by choice at age 25 and wrote his first symphony at age 28.

Sir William Lawrence Bragg was the youngest person to win a Nobel Prize (for physics) at age 25.

At the age of 26, Yet Another Hierarchical Officious Oracle (Yahoo!) David Filo and Jerry Yang, Ph.D. candidates in electrical engineering at Stanford University, started their guide in a campus trailer to keep track of their personal interests.

Einstein was 26 when he showed how mass and energy were equivalent $E=MC^2$.

YEAR 25

Start taking a daily multivitamin.

YEAR 30

Give to charities or social causes.

In 1877, at age 30, Thomas Edison invented the phonograph.

The brain contains about 100 billion neurons, which begin to die at the rate of thousands each day sometime after age 30 and are never replaced.

At age 30, Sylvester Stallone wrote *Rocky* in three days. It sold for a nominal fee with the stipulation that he would star in the film. The movie went on to gross over $100 million and won the Oscar for best picture.

Age at which people must be put to death for population control in the movie *Logan's Run*.

YEARS 35–55

Best age for plastic surgery: Skin becomes less firm and elastic as we age; younger patients can expect better results than older patients.

YEAR 40

Start testing for prostate cancer.

Every woman over age 40 should get an annual mammogram.

Gordie Howe scored the most points (103) in his 26-year NHL career at the age of 41.

George Foreman won the heavyweight champion title in boxing in 1994 at age 46.

YEAR 40

Get all your recommended medical tests: glaucoma, prostrate cancer, and so on.

Take a year sabbatical and travel the world.

Write your midlife autobiography, even just for yourself.

YEAR 48

8 things to do before you retire:

1. Determine your retirement expenses.

2. Review your insurance coverage.

3. Note Medicare milestones on your calendar.

4. Know when to apply for your Social Security benefits.

5. Develop a retirement income plan.

6. Select pension benefits and 401(k) distribution options.

7. Review wills, trusts, powers of attorney, and beneficiaries.

8. Set aside emergency funds.

Eat high fiber cereal (at least 7 grams per serving) and put some blueberries on that cereal.

Drink tea: tea has more antioxidants than most vegetables. People who drink four cups of green tea a day seem to get less cancer, perhaps due to a powerful antioxidant called EGCG. Black tea contains quercetin, a compound that helps prevent blood clots—the immediate triggers of most heart attacks.

50s

You should feel free to make changes at midlife. These changes will help you to navigate successfully through the next half of your life.

Expand your identity. Be the unique individual that you are.

Increase physical activity.

Maintain a youthful mind and a positive outlook.

60s

Get another degree.

Be constantly creative; exercise your brain as well as your body.

Never stop working. Retirement is a fallacy.

Hang out with people of all ages, don't surround yourself with people your age.

70s

Protecting and nurturing your emotional well-being is as important, if not more important, than taking care of your physical body.

Contact with others, whether it be at work, church activities, or family get-togethers, will feed your spirit and can provide purpose and meaning in your life.

Further, social involvement can help combat loneliness and depression and keep you active physically. So make friends and meet new people!

100s

Some facts (from the New England Centenarian Study, Harvard, The Minnesota Nun Study, the University of Georgia Centenarian Study):

Centenarians are not obese.

Centenarians rarely smoke.

Centenarians seem to have delayed or avoided age-related health problems such as stroke, heart attacks, cancer, diabetes although no one knows why (many Centenarians are donating their bodies to science for study after their deaths).

Centenarians have a stress-reduction mindset—they handle stress better than others (sometimes called the "Centenarian Personality").

Centenarians have a sense of humor—an ability to laugh at themselves and others.

Centenarians have a sense of hope—they look forward to tomorrow with anticipation.

Centenarians are engaged—they do something, have an interest, are involved.

Centenarians have an ability to cope with loss (the longer you live, the more you lose: family, including children, friends, sight, hearing, driving, etc.) and still go on with life.

Madame Jeanne Calment, from Arles in France, had the most reliable claim to be the longest lived individual in the world. She was born on February 21, 1875 and died August 4, 1997 at the age of 122.

Be HERE.

CONCLUSION

Now that you have the tools, be like a designer approaching a new project. Assess the matter at hand and come up with proposals. You might even want to develop three or four for each issue and weigh out the solutions until you come to the right one.

In design, there is something called **reverse engineering**. You take an existing project and you strip it down to see the pros and cons, and see what works and what doesn't work. You can also take it from there.

As we have seen, you can do that with the world around you. Look at the people you know, analyze them, see what works and doesn't

Be NOW.

work in their lives. Try to figure out why. **Become a student of the human condition. Read biographies and autobiographies.** You can learn so much about life by studying the lives around you, those that are still here, and those that are long gone. A book about a person's life gives you valuable insight into what worked for them. If you focus on these matters, you can develop a kind of strategy of life, a vision of what works for you, the things you respond to, and the life you want to design for yourself.

DO CONFORM.

N'T

Be responsible
for achieving your own dreams.

They should teach a class on designing your self in elementary school. In that class, you would learn all about navigating the world, all the ups and downs. Instead of waiting for life to happen to us, we would make life happen. Instead of being surprised by setbacks, we would be better prepared for them and know how to handle them.

The most critical lesson is to live in the present. The past is pointless; here and now is all we've got. Living in the present is not an excuse for not planning your future; it is simply a way of learning to enjoy the moment. Living in the present is to have a grasp and control over your destiny. You make it happen. Take charge—it's up to you.

As you move into the future, leave something significant behind. Make your mark on the world. Whether it's a creation or a child, if they grow up to do wonderful things, you've improved the world. When we leave something behind, we are made immortal in some small way. So leave something behind that's part of you. Your life is your own movie to write and direct. Make it your very best design.

Be here and be now.

Focus on the present to manage the future. Not vice versa. Think about now and not "what if . . ." If you haven't already, read Eckhart Tolle's *The Power of Now*.

We are always thinking. We don't seem to have the ability to live in the moment. That's where meditation comes in. You try to stop the rush of the brain and create a void where you can just be. You step out of yourself into nothingness and freedom. An unquiet mind is all over the place.

Let go of the ego. Completely.
I have always been amazed at how easily people accept defeat, and I have never really understood it. If you look closely at some of the successful people you know, you will likely find one common character trait: They are fighters. The people who fail are the ones who give up at the first sign of difficulty. They are brought down by self-defeating thoughts. *I can't. I'm not smart enough. I'm not talented enough.* If you begin to believe this, you are lost. We all have talent. We are all creative.

There are no problems, only opportunities.
As actors say, "fake it till you make it." If they're not sure about a role, they just plunge in and act as if they know what they're doing and they eventually find their way. They believe in themselves, and their ability and that attitude gets them there.

Attitude is clarity. Tell yourself that success is around the corner.

Focus. Decide what your goal is. Establish priorities for your life.

Be your own person. Don't conform.
Be responsible for achieving your own dreams.
Laziness is the Antichrist.

Viktor Frankl, who survived life at Auschwitz, the death camp, and went on to become a famous psychoanalyst, had this to say:

Think of yourself in new terms.

"Everything can be taken from a man but one thing; the last of the human freedoms—to choose one's attitude in any given set of circumstances, to choose one's own way."

He kept fighting. He didn't take no for answer. He expected the best from himself, even when there was no hope left. We have it very easy.

Don't be afraid to fail—everyone does.
Don't be afraid of rejection—you'll get plenty.
Start thinking of yourself in the right terms. For example, if you don't get a job you really wanted, you feel like a loser. You're not a loser. You simply didn't get a job. Why are you letting a minor setback color your entire life?

Stop defining yourself in terms of negative images. If you think you're a lazy person, you'll accept that as your true self. If you learn to define yourself in more positive terms, you'll not only come to believe it, you could become that person. Self-pity is deadly.

Stop playing the same old song. A lot of people are stuck on the same track. Change it. Listen to a new song. If you keep living in the past, dwelling on past failures, you'll stay there. You need to get rid of that to improve your present performance. Not all of us are going to succeed. Not all of us are destined for greatness. But we can get the life we design for ourselves.

Learn to accept your shortcomings. None of us is perfect.
Don't dwell on your weaknesses—work on your strengths.
Try to **be more tolerant** of yourself. And, while you're at it, be more tolerant of other people: They are struggling, and they have flaws, too.

Celebrate
your individuality.

People can be pretty screwed up, but if you look for it, you can find something to like in just about everyone.

Don't beat yourself up over setbacks or perceived failures.
When you're down, you're more susceptible to life's unfairness.

A friend of mine was on antidepressants. He said something very revealing once. He said that the drugs didn't change the world, they only changed the way he responded to the world. They helped him be less depressed. He realized that the world was still there, and that it hadn't changed. The only thing that had changed, thanks to the antidepressant, was the way he responded to it. When he figured this out, he tossed the drugs and changed his attitude.

When you're up and feeling good about yourself, you're less likely to be affected by setbacks. **So stop criticizing yourself.** Stop wondering whether you should have done this or that or how things would have turned out if you had acted differently in a certain situation. There's nothing to be gained from that type of behavior. You're living in a past you can't undo, and no amount of worrying is going to change it.

Get the job done: Aim for that finish line.

True success comes from the inside. Redesign yourself and you'll succeed. Think of yourself in new terms.

Did you know that the word *habit* used to refer to your clothes? A habit is literally something that is "worn" by your personality. Think of habits as clothes and you'll go into the closet and discover how easy it is to change them.

Learn to be yourself. Celebrate your individuality. Appreciate the things that set you apart. Find out who you are, embrace that person, and find out what you want.

It's amazing how powerful the mind is. To say you can do anything you set your mind to do sounds like a cliché, but it's true. You have to train yourself to see the world in a different way, to see the possibilities. Sometimes it's good to start fresh. It's like cleaning the hard drive on your computer—it can make you more efficient, effective, free to be more creative. Clear out the junk. Start listening to what you want and go for it!

You really *can* redesign your life. And you can do it one day at a time. What do you hope to accomplish this morning? By the end of the day? By the end of the month? By the end of year?

In five years? And so on . . .

You have more control over your life than you realize. In fact, you're the only one in control. Design is about control, setting up a program, criteria, a mandate. If you think about your mind and life in the same terms, you will take successful control of your life.

The first thing to do is to draft the program:

This is my life and this is what I want.

This is my life and this is what it could be.

YOU CAN

redesign your life.

DESIGN YOUR SELF. Copyright 2006 by Karim Rashid. All rights reserved. Printed in China. No part of this book may be used or reproduced in any manner whatsoever without written permission except in the case of brief quotations embodied in critical articles and reviews. For information, address HarperCollins Publishers Inc., 10 East 53rd Street, New York, NY 10022.

HarperCollins books may be purchased for educational, business, or sales promotional use. For information please write: Special Markets Department, HarperCollins Publishers Inc., 10 East 53rd Street, New York, NY 10022.

FIRST EDITION

Book and cover design: Stephen Schmidt / Duuplex

Printed on acid-free paper

Library of Congress Cataloging-in-Publication Data
Rashid, Karim, 1960–
Design your self: rethinking the way you live, love, work, and play /
Karim Rashid.—1st ed. p. cm.
ISBN-13: 978-0-06-083902-4
ISBN-10: 0-06-083902-3
1. Home economics. 2. Life skills. 3. Quality of life. 4.
Design, Industrial. I. Title.
TX147.R37 2006
640—dc22   2005051417
06 07 08 09 10 IM 10 9 8 7 6 5 4 3 2 1